# Language Arts
## Workbook

Siegfried Engelmann
Bernadette Kelly
Susie Andrist
Jerry Silbert

## Acknowledgments

The authors are grateful to the following people for their assistance in the preparations of Reading Mastery Transformations Grade 3 Language.

Amilcar Cifuentes
Gary Davis
Cally Dwyer
Katherine Gries
Debbi Kleppen
Margie Mayo
Patricia McFadden
Melissa Morrow

Trevor Smith
Leta Tillitt
Piper VanNortwick
John Weber
Tina Wells
Nancy Woolfson
Mary Rosenbaum

**PHOTO CREDITS**
**020** Ariel Skelley/Blend Images LLC; **036** Monkey Business Images/Shutterstock; **040** Steve Debenport/E+/Getty Images; **067** dolgachov/123RF; **068** Hero Images Inc./Alamy Stock Photo; **095** Andrew Olney/age fotostock; **111** Sam Edwards/Glow Images; **115** Rido/Shutterstock; **131** Digital Vision/Alamy; **133** Maica/E+/Getty Images; **137** Alexey Ivanov/123RF; **139** Alexander Spatari/Moment/Getty Images; **140** Alamy Stock Photo; **173** Design Pics Inc./Alamy Images; **176** Ingram Publishing; **180** flairmicro/123RF; **184** (l)Juice Images/Alamy, (r)PeopleImages/E+/Getty Images; **187** John Giustina/Photodisc/Getty Images; **191** Elena Blokhina/123RF; **195** Ingram Publishing; **196** incamerastock/Alamy Stock Photo; **207** Viacheslav Iakobchuk/Alamy Stock Photo; **208** Michael Reusse/Westend61/Getty Images; **211** (l)NASA/Johns Hopkins University Applied Physics Laboratory/Carnegie Institution of Washington, (cl)JPL/NASA, (cr)Stocktrek Images, Inc./Alamy Stock Photo, (r)Steve Lee (University of Colorado), Jim Bell (Cornell University), Mike Wolff (Space Science Institute), and NASA; **212** Meinzahn/iStockphoto/Getty Images; **215** (tl)Marc Romanelli/Blend Images LLC, (tr)Aaron Flaum/Alamy Images, (bl)I. Rozenbaum & F. Cirou/PhotoAlto, (br)Anthony Harvie/DigitalVision/Getty Images; **221** (l)Somchai Som/Shutterstock, (cl)epantha/iStock/Getty Images, (cr)Shutterstock/nimon, (r)Ingram Publishing/SuperStock; **222** wavebreakmedia/Shutterstock; **224** Irina_Gulyaeva/Shutterstock; **227** Gabi Moisa/Shutterstock.

**MT08 05** Alexey Ivanov/123RF; **MT14 02** (l)wavebreakmedia/Shutterstock; **MT02 004** McGraw-Hill Education.

mheducation.com/prek-12

Copyright © 2021 McGraw-Hill Education

All rights reserved. No part of this publication may be reproduced or distributed in any form or by any means, or stored in a database or retrieval system, without the prior written consent of McGraw-Hill Education, including, but not limited to, network storage or transmission, or broadcast for distance learning.

Permission is granted to reproduce the material contained on pages T-1–T-10 on the condition that such material be reproduced only for classroom use; be provided to students, teachers, or families without charge; and be used solely in conjunction with *Reading Mastery Transformations*.

Send all inquiries to:
McGraw-Hill Education
8787 Orion Place
Columbus, OH 43240

ISBN: 978-0-07-905373-2
MHID: 0-07-905373-4

Printed in the United States of America.

3 4 5 6 7 8 9 10 LMN 26 25 24 23 22

Name _____

**A** Circle **reports** or **does not report**.

1. The boy was from New York.  —  reports    does not report

2. A boy sat on the dock and fished.  —  reports    does not report

3. The boy wanted to be a boxer.  —  reports    does not report

4. The girl wore a blue life jacket.  —  reports    does not report

5. The girl sat in an inner tube.  —  reports    does not report

6. The girl liked to swim.  —  reports    does not report

7. The water was very warm.  —  reports    does not report

8. Some fish fell out of the bucket.  —  reports    does not report

## B  Write the word that tells what happened.

1. jump _____
2. pull _____
3. bark _____

4. push _____
5. pick _____
6. burn _____

## C  Write the word that tells what happened.

1. find    found
2. give    gave
3. buy     bought
4. dig     dug
5. has     had

6. buy  _____
7. find _____
8. dig  _____
9. has  _____
10. give _____

Lesson 1

**D** Complete each sentence.

1. _____ came into the room

2. _____ stood behind his desk

3. _____ made marks on a piece of paper

4. _____ watched the alligator from the front row

**E** Circle the part of each sentence that names.

1. An old cowboy went to town.
2. That cowboy rode his horse to town.
3. He went to town to buy food.
4. He rode his horse to the food store.
5. The cowboy went inside.
6. He bought the food that they needed.

**END OF LESSON 1**

## 2

**Name** _____

**A** Circle *reports* or *does not report*.

1. Mrs. Lee talked to her sister. — reports / does not report
2. The baby sat on a rug. — reports / does not report
3. The baby had just learned how to walk. — reports / does not report
4. The cat reached toward the birdcage. — reports / does not report
5. The cat was seven years old. — reports / does not report
6. The dog liked to play with the baby. — reports / does not report
7. The baby held on to the dog's tail. — reports / does not report
8. Mrs. Lee was making a birthday cake. — reports / does not report

**B** **Circle the part of each sentence that names.**

A little gray cat looked for its owner. It looked and looked.

The poor gray cat was hungry. The cat made a lot of noise.

It went up one street and down another. The cat found its owner.

The little cat felt very happy.

**C** **Complete each item with He, She, or It.**

1. The car broke down.  _____ broke down.

2. The dream went on for an hour.  _____ went on for an hour.

3. The young boy sat in a chair.  _____ sat in a chair.

4. The monkey was laughing.  _____ was laughing.

5. My older sister helped me.  _____ helped me.

6. The pen fell off the table.  _____ fell off the table.

**D** Change each sentence so it tells what happened.

| drank | drove | ate | played | ran |

1. The boy was eating lunch.

2. The girl is running home.

3. The boy was playing soccer.

4. He is drinking water.

5. She was driving a bus.

**E** Copy each sentence on lined paper.

E

1. Maria and her sister went to the store.

2. My friend had a cold.

3. The class went to the lunchroom.

4. His bike had a flat tire.

**END OF LESSON 2**

Name _____

**A** Circle reports or does not report.

1. The boys were in a garage.  reports   does not report

2. The monkey should be in a zoo.  reports   does not report

3. Harry was working with his brother.  reports   does not report

4. The monkey grabbed the toolbox.  reports   does not report

5. The monkey was 5 years old.  reports   does not report

6. The bike belonged to Harry.  reports   does not report

7. Bert held onto the handlebars.  reports   does not report

8. Bert's mother was in the kitchen.  reports   does not report

## B  Complete each item with He, She, or It.

1. The shirt was covered with dirt.

   _____ was covered with dirt.

2. The rubber ball fell off the table.

   _____ fell off the table.

3. The man sat in a chair.

   _____ sat in a chair.

4. The young woman rode a bike.

   _____ rode a bike.

5. The book was very funny.

   _____ was very funny.

6. The game ended at four o'clock.

   _____ ended at four o'clock.

## C  Change each sentence so it tells what happened.

| built | folded | licked | looked | sat | took |

1. He was taking a bath.

2. They were looking at the sky.

3. The dog was licking my face.

4. She is building a fire.

5. The teacher was sitting on a chair.

6. She is folding the paper.

**D** **Circle the part of each sentence that names.**

An old red bike sat in the yard for years. That bike became rusty. It had spider webs on the wheels. A girl decided to fix up the bike. She painted the bike bright red. She put new tires on the bike. The bike looked great. The girl liked the bike.

**E** **Copy the paragraph.**

Pedro had a very smart dog. The dog could do many tricks. It could walk on its back legs. It could jump through a hoop. All the children liked to play with the smart dog.

**END OF LESSON 3**

# 4   Name _____

## A   Circle the part of each sentence that names.

A hungry little cat walked into a restaurant. It wanted something to eat. A nice woman owned the restaurant. She gave the cat a bowl of milk. The little animal drank every drop of milk. The woman liked the cat. She made a little bed for it. The cat had a new home.

## B   Complete each item with He, It, or They.

1. The man and the woman ate lunch.     _____ ate lunch.

2. Latrell and Kedrick walked on the sand.     _____ walked on the sand.

3. The truck had a flat tire.     _____ had a flat tire.

4. The apples cost 84 cents.     _____ cost 84 cents.

5. The women wore red shirts.     _____ wore red shirts.

6. The old book was worth a lot of money.     _____ was worth a lot of money.

7. Alberto and his dog went jogging.     _____ went jogging.

8. The old man wore a long blue coat.     _____ wore a long blue coat.

**C** Change each sentence so it tells what happened.

| held | painted | rode | stood | talked | washed |

1. She is riding a horse.

2. The girls were talking loudly.

3. Four men are painting the room.

4. He was holding the baby.

5. She is standing on a chair.

6. They were washing the windows.

**D** Copy the paragraph.

> Jason had a bad day. He missed breakfast because he woke up late. He had to walk to school in the rain.

**Check CP:** Does each sentence begin with a capital letter and end with a period?

**Check SP:** Did you spell all the words correctly?

**E** Circle the sentence that tells what the person did.

1.

The firefighter is chopping a hole in the door.

The firefighter was chopping a hole in the door.

The firefighter chopped a hole in the door.

2.

Sally is diving into the pool.

Sally dove into the pool.

Sally was diving into the pool.

3.

Latrell ate a sandwich.

Latrell was eating a sandwich.

Latrell is eating a sandwich.

4.

The girl was painting the wall.

The girl is painting the wall.

The girl painted the wall.

**END OF LESSON 4**

**A** **Capitalize the names.**

We saw carol beasley and her mother at the baseball game. I asked carol if they had moved yet. Her mother said that they were moving next week. Then my friend billy lopez said that he could help carol and her mother when they moved. That made me mad because billy never helped me or dave.

**B** **Circle the subject of each sentence.**

1. Three older boys went to the store.

2. A horse and a dog went to a stream.

3. A man sat on a log.

4. They sat on a bench.

5. My friend and his mother were hungry.

6. My hands and my face got dirty.

## C  Change each sentence so it tells what happened.

| sat | threw | rubbed | wore | cleaned |

1. They were wearing helmets.

2. She was throwing the ball.

3. They were cleaning the room.

4. The boys were sitting on the floor.

5. He was wearing a new shirt.

6. The clown was rubbing his nose.

## D  Complete each item with He, She, It, or They.

1. A cat and a dog made a mess.          _____ made a mess.

2. The girls went to school.             _____ went to school.

3. My mother is very pretty.             _____ is very pretty.

4. Rodney and his brother were not home. _____ were not home.

5. Four ducks swam on the lake.          _____ swam on the lake.

6. The tables were old.                  _____ were old.

7. My brother came home late.            _____ came home late.

8. That car was bright red.              _____ was bright red.

**E** Fix the passage so no sentences begin with And or And then.

A bull chased Pam through a field. Pam jumped over a fence. And then the bull jumped over the fence. And Pam kept on running. And the bull was right behind her. Pam ran over to a tree. And then she climbed up the tree as fast as she could. And the bull waited under the tree until the sun went down. And then Pam climbed down after the bull left. And she knew she shouldn't have taken a shortcut through that field.

**F** Circle the sentence that tells what the person did.

Norma was sawing a board.

Norma is sawing a board.

Norma sawed a board.

Yancy was trying to ride a bull.

Yancy tried to ride a bull.

Yancy is trying to ride a bull.

**END OF LESSON 5**

Lesson 5   15

**A** **Capitalize the names in this paragraph.**

Part of the warren family lived in utah. Another part lived in virginia. They decided to get together at a place between the two states. They finally decided to meet in chicago, illinois. They thought chicago was a good choice because it was a large city that had good places to go like brookfield zoo and wrigley park. arnold warren and his family didn't have to go very far because they lived in evanston, illinois. evanston is only a few miles from chicago.

**B** **Circle the subject of each sentence.**

1. Two lazy dogs walked through the park.

2. She looked at the swans.

3. Their cat was 11 years old.

4. Sam and his father could not agree.

5. It was cold.

6. My sister is very pretty.

## C  Change each sentence so it tells what happened.

| took | chased | wrote | ate | washed |

1. A dog was chasing my brother.

2. The girl was washing the car.

3. He was writing a letter.

4. She was eating apples.

5. The airplane was taking off.

## D  Write He, She, or It in each blank.

1. Robert spent all morning cleaning his room. _____ put his dirty clothes into the laundry basket. _____ washed the floor and the windows.

2. My sister went to the park. _____ played basketball with her friends for two hours. _____ scored 20 points.

3. The boat sailed on a lake for two hours. _____ had three sails. _____ moved very quickly across the water.

**END OF LESSON 6**

**7**   Name _____

**A**   **Circle the subject of each sentence.**

1. My old blue phone doesn't work.

2. The weatherman said that it would rain soon.

3. Mr. Anderson and his brother live in that house.

4. The cow almost fell over.

5. I could not see through the fog.

6. Roland's mother makes great pizza.

**B**   **Change each sentence so it tells what happened.**

| painted | told | sat | washed | picked |

1. The men were telling jokes.

2. She was picking up the pencils.

3. They were washing the car.

4. He was sitting on a log.

5. She was painting the wall.

Lesson 7

## C. Cross out some of the names and write He, She, or It.

<sup>a</sup>Marvin found many things when he went walking. <sup>b</sup>Marvin once found a striped cat. <sup>c</sup>That cat was very thin. <sup>d</sup>That cat was sitting on the sidewalk. <sup>e</sup>Marvin took the cat home with him. <sup>f</sup>Marvin tried to hide the cat from his mother. <sup>g</sup>His mother heard the cat. <sup>h</sup>His mother liked the cat and told Marvin that he could keep it.

## D. Capitalize the names in each sentence.

1. Last may, I went to river city with nancy and mrs. briggs.
2. Joe asked dr. morris to speak to our class on tuesday.
3. Emily green had a horse named jennie.
4. My brother steve rode jennie from rosetown to jasper.
5. Next sunday will be the last day in january.

**E** Fix the passage so that no sentences begin with <u>And</u> or <u>And then</u>.

Tom threw a snowball at his friend. And it hit his friend's leg. And then his friend chased him. And they both ran as fast as they could. His friend caught Tom in the middle of the park. And then Tom told his friend that he was sorry for hitting him in the leg with the snowball. The boys shook hands. And they were still friends.

**END OF LESSON 7**

Name _____

**A** **Circle the subject of each sentence.**

1. A jet airplane made a lot of noise.

2. A man and his dog went walking.

3. He ate lunch in the office.

4. My brother and his friend played in the park.

5. A little cat drank milk.

**B** **Circle each subject. Put in the missing capital letters and periods.**

A young boy threw a ball the ball went over his friend's head it rolled into the street a big truck ran over the ball the truck driver gave the boys a new ball they thanked the truck driver

**C** **Cross out some of the names and write He, She, or It.**

[a]Trina loved to look for things on the sidewalk. [b]Trina found three bugs, two rocks, and a baseball. [c]Her father did not like some of the things she found. [d]Her father did not like the bugs that Trina brought home. [e]Trina's brother liked one of the things Trina found. [f]Trina's brother liked the baseball.

### D. Fix the passage so that no sentences begin with And or And then.

Richard had a good day. Richard's teacher gave him his report card just before the school day ended. And Richard jumped with joy when he saw the good marks on his report card. And then he ran home to show his mother the report card. And then he gave her the report card. And then his mother read the report card for several minutes. And she was so happy that she made Richard and his sister a big pizza for dinner.

# INDEPENDENT WORK

### E. Capitalize the names in these sentences.

1. Mrs. hess will take us to the portland zoo next monday.

2. Jerry showed tonya and ellen his pictures from washington.

3. Last saturday, corrina found a kitten.

4. When mr. adams got home on thursday, he watched the news.

5. Ramon and james were both born in december.

**END OF LESSON 8**

**Name** _____

**A** **Put in the missing capital letters and periods.**

a boy took his mom to the movies he had

a good time the movie was very funny his mom

bought a big box of popcorn they rode home on

their bikes

**B** **Change the passage so that all the sentences tell what happened.**

Marcus woke up late. He was running down the stairs. He grabbed his school book. He is jumping on his bike. He rode the bike as fast as he could. He was parking the bike. He ran into the classroom. He was sitting in his chair.

**C** **Cross out some of the names and write He, She, or It.**

Ted had a birthday yesterday. Ted was 11 years old. His mother brought a big birthday cake to school. His mother gave a piece of cake to each person in Ted's class. The cake tasted great. The cake had chocolate icing.

Lesson 9

## D  Use the checks to edit the passage.

tonya jackson was playing baseball. And her team was losing three to one. tonya was at bat. The pitcher threw the ball to tonya. tonya swung. She missed the ball. And tonya was mad. The pitcher threw the ball again. And then Tonya swung. She hit the ball. And it went far over everybody's head. Tonya ran around the bases. Her team won the game. And then all the girls clapped for tonya.

**Check AND:** Do any sentences begin with **and** or **and then**? AND _____

**Check N:** Does each part of a person's name begin with a capital letter? N _____

# INDEPENDENT WORK

## E  Capitalize the names in these sentences.

1. Next thursday, josh is taking me to new york.

2. Shanna plays basketball at the gym on the corner of northridge and main street.

3. My sister had a dog named elvis and a cat named elroy.

4. We watched the lakers play in los angeles.

5. Last february, ms. keller went to times square.

**END OF LESSON 9**

**A** **Edit the passage so it tells what happened.**

Jerry heard a noise. He was seeing a little kitten on the sidewalk. He picked up the kitten. He was taking it home with him. He was giving it some water. He made a little bed for it. He loved his new pet.

**B** **Put in the missing capital letters and periods.**

a girl threw a ball to her brother she threw the ball too hard it rolled into the street the boy started to run into the street a truck moved toward the boy a woman saw the truck she grabbed the boy the truck ran over the ball the woman told the boy to be more careful

**C** **Use the checks to edit the paragraph.**

A woman lived near our school Her name was mrs. jones she was an airplane pilot. She told us many stories about flying planes

**Check CP:** Does each sentence begin with a capital letter and end with a period?
CP _____

**Check N:** Does each part of a person's name begin with a capital letter?
N _____

**D** **Cross out some of the names and write He, It, or They.**

The play began almost an hour late. The play was supposed to start at 6 o'clock. People started clapping when it was 15 minutes late. Then they began shouting. Then other people shouted, "Stop yelling!" The owner of the theater finally came on to the stage. The owner told us that some wires had burned up, but they were getting fixed. The show started at 6:50 p.m. The show was very funny. Everybody shouted and clapped and cheered. Everybody thought it was worth the wait.

# INDEPENDENT WORK

**E** **Capitalize the names in these sentences.**

1. We went to the movies every saturday when I was young.

2. Evelyn's family went to yellowstone national park.

3. In june, tina camped in the back yard.

4. I called my cousin in chicago, illinois.

5. Jerome's mom took him to dr. keen on madison street.

**F** **Write the missing word for each item. Use an apostrophe.**

1. the cup that belongs to the man

   the _____ cup

2. the leg that belongs to that horse

   that _____ leg

3. the skirt that belongs to my sister

   my _____ skirt

4. the house that belongs to our friend

   our _____ house

**END OF LESSON 10**

Lesson 10   27

## 11

**A** Write V above the words that are verbs.

1. cried
2. buy
3. house
4. whispered
5. teacher
6. yellow
7. swim

**B** Put in the missing capital letters and periods.

a man took a big egg out of a nest. The man brought the egg to his house he thought that the egg might be worth a lot of money. The doorbell rang the man walked to the door. He opened the door a big bird flew into the room. It picked up the egg the man fainted. The big bird flew away with the egg

**C** **Change the passage so it tells what happened.**

Shameka bought a little tree. She was digging a hole in her yard. She put the tree into the hole. She was filling the hole with dirt. She was watering the tree. She built a little fence around the tree.

**D** **Complete each item. Use an apostrophe.**

1. The pencil belonged to **a girl.** The pencil was yellow.
   _____ was yellow.

2. The nest belonged to **that bird.** The nest had eggs in it.
   _____ had eggs in it.

3. The glasses belonged to **my friend.** The glasses were broken.
   _____ were broken.

4. The bottle belonged to **her baby.** The bottle had milk in it.
   _____ had milk in it.

**E** **Circle the subject and underline the predicate.**

1. Five cats were on the roof.
2. They read two funny books.
3. A red bird landed on a roof.
4. A dog and a cat played in their yard.
5. It stopped.

# INDEPENDENT WORK

**F** **Capitalize the names in these sentences.**

1. Next tuesday, our class will watch a movie about spain.

2. Ivana's favorite months are july and august.

3. During the summer, the warren family drove across the united states.

4. On saturday, jake will fly to canada.

5. We buy our groceries at ray's on main street.

**G** **Edit the passage so some sentences start with He, She, or They.**

Jodi was the fastest girl on the team. Jodi could run faster than everyone else. The boys tried to catch her in the longest race. The boys finished far behind her. Jodi sat on the grass when the race was over. Jodi's dad was proud of her. Jodi's dad took a photo of her winning the race. Jodi was the happiest girl at the meet.

**END OF LESSON 11**

**Name** _____

**A** **Write V above the words that are verbs.**

1. went    2. birds    3. walks    4. flew    5. pretty

6. sleeps    7. sold    8. book    9. tall

**B** **Circle the subject and underline the predicate.**

1. Sara and Harry painted the kitchen blue.

2. Sara had a paintbrush.

3. Harry used a roller.

4. They stopped to eat lunch.

5. She laughed.

6. The windows were blue.

Lesson 12

## C  Complete each item. Use an apostrophe.

1. The car belonged to **Tom.** The car was new.

   _____ was new.

2. The wheel belonged to **his bike.** The wheel was bent.

   _____ was bent.

3. The motor belonged to **that truck.** The motor made a lot of noise.

   _____ made a lot of noise.

4. The finger belonged to **Sally.** The finger was swollen.

   _____ was swollen.

5. The mouth belonged to **the dog.** The mouth was sore.

   _____ was sore.

**END OF LESSON 12**

**Name** _____

### A  Write the missing sentence.

1. Ellen

2. Bonnie

3.

4.

| | |
|---|---|
| | Ellen loved breakfast. She ate her eggs, toast, and bacon slowly. She met Bonnie on her way to the bus stop and talked for a |
| IH | while. ∧ Ellen had to walk to school. She got to school late. |

Lesson 13   33

**B** Write the verb that tells what happened.

1. begins  _____
2. brings  _____
3. flies  _____
4. swims  _____
5. takes  _____
6. comes  _____

**C** Circle the subject and underline the predicate.

1. Mr. Turner and his son went fishing at Trout Lake.
2. The woman in the red hat lives on the next block.
3. It fell.
4. They loved to sing old songs.

**D** Write V above the words that are verbs.

1. buy
2. smiled
3. kind
4. tall
5. kicks
6. went
7. boy

## E  Use the check letters to edit the paragraph.

|  |  |
|---|---|
|  | Mrs. Clancy took a roast out of the oven. |
| **DID** | She is putting it on the table. Her dog Rex |
| **IH** | wanted to eat that roast. ∧ Rex went over to the |
|  | table. He took a bite out of the roast, but it was |
|  | very hot. Rex started to howl. Mrs. Clancy ran |
| **CP** | back to the kitchen that was the last time Rex |
| **DID** | tries to eat something that was on the table. |

**Check IH:** Did you tell the important things that happened?

**Check CP:** Does each sentence begin with a capital letter and end with a period?

**Check DID:** Does each sentence tell what somebody or something **did?**

**END OF LESSON 13**

# 14  Name _____

## INDEPENDENT WORK

**A** Label the five words that are verbs.

1. drinks     2. pretty     3. fat      4. played

5. silly      6. gives      7. sat      8. girl

9. car        10. ate

**B** Circle the subject of each sentence.

1. My little brother is cute.
2. We ride the bus home every day.
3. That black cat belongs to me.
4. They flew to Montana for a vacation.
5. Their books got wet in the rain.

**END OF LESSON 14**

**Name** _____

## A  Circle the subject. Underline the predicate. Then label the verb.

1. (Six bottles) <u>were on the table.</u>  [V above "were"]

2. An old lion chased the rabbit.

3. Jane and Sue sat under a tree.

4. His brother had a candy bar.

## B  Fix the mistakes.

1. the boys goed to Bills house.  (3)

2. Alice fell asleep she was very tired.  (2)

3. that boys shirt has six red buttons and four yellow buttons  (3)

4. My best friends are jerry gomez and alex jordan.  (4)

5. Melissa and richard put their dog on richards bed.  (3)

6. We looked outside the rain had just stopped.  (2)

Lesson 15

## C. Use the checks to fix the mistakes.

|     |     |
| --- | --- |
|     | At 7 o'clock Maria's car broke down. |
| CP  | smoke came out of the engine, and the car |
| IH  | would not run. ∧ At 7:45 the truck arrived. Joe |
| DID | was the driver. Maria tells Joe what happened. |
|     | Joe hooked up the car to the tow truck. At |
|     | 8:15 Maria got in the tow truck and they drove |
| CP  | to the shop. they arrived at the shop at 8:45 |

**Check IH:** Did you tell all the important things that happened?

**Check CP:** Does each sentence begin with a capital letter and end with a period?

**Check DID:** Does each sentence tell what somebody or something **did**?

END OF LESSON 15

Name _____

**A** Write the two-word verb for each item.

1. pushed _____

2. started _____

3. filled _____

4. burned _____

5. tricked _____

6. jumped _____

**B** Fix the mistakes in each sentence.

1. My dads cat had four kittens  (2)

2. She teached robert and jerry how to ride a bike.  (3)

3. she washed the windows of her moms car  (3)

4. We seen mr. jordan in the store he waved to us.  (5)

5. gingers paper had more mistakes than franks paper.  (4)

END OF LESSON 16

**A** Circle the subject and underline the predicate. Then label the verb.

1. The oldest boy walked to the store.

2. The oldest boy was walking to the store.

3. Two girls ate lunch.

4. Two girls were eating lunch.

5. A fish swam in the bathtub.

6. A fish was swimming in the bathtub.

**B** Use the check letters to edit the paragraph.

| | |
|---|---|
| **DID** | Greg had a birthday party. Greg is opening his presents at the table. His mom lit the candles on his |
| **CP** | cake. then his mom carried the cake to the table. |
| **IH** | Everybody sang Happy Birthday to Greg. Next, Greg cut the cake. His mom gave pieces to his friends. Julius |
| **DID** | says the cake was very tasty. |

**Check IH:** Did you tell all the important things that happened?

**Check CP:** Does each sentence begin with a capital letter and end with a period?

**Check DID:** Does each sentence tell what somebody or something **did**?

### C  Circle the subject. Then underline the predicate.

1. He went to the store <u>after dinner</u>.

2. She fell asleep <u>before the movie ended</u>.

3. A bird started to sing <u>early in the morning</u>.

4. The boy cleaned the garage after breakfast.

5. Ann fixed her car yesterday.

6. All the people clapped when the movie ended.

## INDEPENDENT WORK

### D  Capitalize the names in these sentences.

1. Jenna named her dog mr. bones.

2. Our new teacher will be mrs. norris.

3. My friend fiona walks to central park every monday.

4. Mr. cheeseman moved to b street in redburn.

5. Winslow's pet rabbits ate all the lettuce in mr. green's garden.

**END OF LESSON 17**

Name _____

**A** Circle the subject and underline the predicate. Then label each verb.

1. The young woman walks to the school.

2. The young woman is walking to the school.

3. The children smile at the clown.

4. The children are smiling at the clown.

5. Mark and Jenny rake the leaves.

6. Mark and Jenny are raking the leaves.

7. They swim in the lake.

8. They are swimming in the lake.

**B** Circle the subject and underline the predicate. Then make a line over the part that tells when.

1. Two trees fell down during the storm.

2. The baby started to cry when his mother left the room.

3. Tom finished his homework at eleven o'clock in the morning.

4. The boy cleaned his room while his mother went shopping.

5. They shook hands after the game.

6. We went to the movies last night.

# INDEPENDENT WORK

**C** Complete each item with **He**, **She**, **It**, or **They**.

1. These worms are red.　　　　　　　_____ are red.

2. Tim Nelson wrote a book.　　　　　_____ wrote a book.

3. Those big boys make a lot of noise.　_____ make a lot of noise.

4. An old lizard lives in that tree.　　　_____ lives in that tree.

5. Hilda lost a front tooth.　　　　　　_____ lost a front tooth.

**END OF LESSON 18**

Name _____

**19**

**A** Add <u>s</u> or <u>es</u> to tell about more than one.

> Does the word end in **s, sh, ch,** or **x?**

1. tool
2. beach
3. crash
4. bowl
5. dish
6. ax
7. swan
8. class

**B** Circle the subject and underline the predicate. Then make a line over the part that tells when.

1. He brushed his teeth after he washed his face.

2. James and Tom did their math in the morning.

3. The engine made a funny noise before the car stopped.

4. Tom read a book while he waited for his brother.

5. Alice and her mother went shopping yesterday afternoon.

6. Our teacher read a story during the lunch hour.

7. The clown climbed the rope when a bell rang.

8. Smoke came from the house after lightning hit it.

**C** Label the verb in each sentence.

1. The boys are riding their bikes.

2. Her mother was singing to herself.

3. They slip on the ice.

4. She was eating in her room.

5. She is sitting on her bed.

6. My brother and sister played in the park.

**D** Use the check letters to edit the paragraph.

| | |
|---|---|
| IH | The rock hit the hornet's nest. Hundreds |
| CP | of hornets came out of the nest. the angry |
| IH | hornets flew toward James. The hornets almost |
| CP | caught him |

**END OF LESSON 19**

**Name** _____

**20**

**A** Add __s__ or __es__ to tell about more than one.

1. leash
2. itch
3. book
4. kiss
5. couch
6. banana
7. icebox
8. clash

**B** Circle the subject and underline the predicate. Then make a line over the part that tells when.

1. Our dog barked when the door opened.

2. We went shopping last night.

3. The girls painted the room while the boys washed the car.

4. Everybody fell asleep after lunch.

5. He held his nose as he jumped into the water.

6. Nobody talked during the movie.

**C** Write an apostrophe for each item that needs one.

1. that mans <u>car</u>
2. two <u>cars</u>
3. many big <u>trees</u>
4. the farmers <u>trees</u>
5. an apples <u>stem</u>
6. the red <u>apples</u>

**END OF LESSON 20**

Lesson 20    47

## 21

**A** Write an apostrophe for each item that needs one.

1. a girls books
2. three small cats
3. those gray clouds
4. my uncles dogs
5. the faster runners
6. the teachers desk

**B** Circle the subject. Underline the predicate. Then make a line over the part that tells when.

1. John went home after the party.
2. After the party, John went home.
3. The girls were tired by the time the sun went down.
4. By the time the sun went down, the girls were tired.
5. The engine made a funny noise before the car stopped.
6. Before the car stopped, the engine made a funny noise.
7. Tammy listened to the radio while Bill did his homework.
8. While Bill did his homework, Tammy listened to the radio.

**END OF LESSON 21**

**A** Circle the subject. Underline the predicate. Then make a line over the part that tells when.

1. Jane got a lot of work done while the baby slept.

   While the baby slept, Jane got a lot of work done.

2. The birds flew south in September.

   In September, the birds flew south.

3. She woke up before the alarm clock rang.

   Before the alarm clock rang, she woke up.

4. He worked on his boat every night.

   Every night, he worked on his boat.

**B** Write an apostrophe for each item that needs one.

1. a womans coat
2. that colts tail
3. the old bucket
4. the books on the shelf
5. a young boys bicycle
6. that books pages
7. the red bicycles

## C  Use the check letters to edit the paragraph.

| | |
|---|---|
| SP | The mother fish grabbed the fishin line in her |
| CP | mouth. The mother fish got angry she swam away |
| | from the boat as fast as she could swim. Jim felt |
| IH | a tug on the fishing line. ^ Rhonda dropped the |
| DID | net and grabs the oars. |

**Check IH:** Did you tell the important things that happened in the middle picture?

**Check CP:** Does each sentence begin with a capital letter and end with a period?

**Check DID:** Does each sentence tell what somebody or something **did**?

**Check SP:** Did you spell words from the word list correctly?

# INDEPENDENT WORK

## D  Add s or es to tell about more than one.

1. lake
2. box
3. paper
4. hiss
5. push
6. dress
7. pan
8. notch

**END OF LESSON 22**

**A** Circle the subject. Underline the predicate. Then make a line over the part that tells when.

1. Jane walked home after school.

   After school, Jane walked home.

2. Tom read a book in the evening.

   In the evening, Tom read a book.

3. The girl rubbed her eyes when the lights came on.

   When the lights came on, the girl rubbed her eyes.

**B** Put in the missing commas.

1. After school Jane walked home.
2. In the evening Tom read a book.
3. When the lights came on the girl rubbed her eyes.

**C** Write an apostrophe for each item that needs one.

1. The old bikes had flat tires.
2. The book's cover was wet.
3. My uncle's farm has cows and horses.
4. Our phones stopped working.
5. Who found my brother's shoes?
6. The books on Rob's desk were new.

## INDEPENDENT WORK

**D** Add s or es to make plural words.

1. ranch
2. mix
3. eye
4. class
5. ash
6. shoe
7. catch
8. gleam

**E** Capitalize the names in these sentences.

1. The gym teacher at madison elementary school will be john rogers.

2. Horace wants to play football for the dallas cowboys in texas.

3. Our waiter's name at jenny's grill is fred.

4. My uncle anthony lives in albany.

5. I walked a block on lincoln street to get to greenway park.

**END OF LESSON 23**

Name _____

24

**A** Underline each subject. Write the pronoun above it.

1. The old man could not start the car.

2. A storm lasted all night.

3. A dog and a cow were eating.

4. The young woman cleaned a table.

5. The trucks went up the hill.

6. A mother held a baby.

**B** Fix the mistakes.

1. Tom said, "why did you do that?  (2)

2. They seen fred and jerry at the store.  (3)

3. Maria said "i love math."  (2)

4. Lisa teached Marys brother to swim.  (2)

5. My sister went to the doctor she had a cold.  (2)

Lesson 24   53

**C** Use the check letters to edit the paragraph.

|     |     |
| --- | --- |
|     | The painter carried his ladder over to |
| CP  | the tree he leaned the ladder against |
| IH  | the tree. ∧ Then Mike picked some apples. He |
| SP  | throow the apples to the painter. The painter |
| DID | put the apples on the ground. Anita unfolds |
| CP  | the blanket she took the food and drinks |
|     | from the basket and put them on the blanket. |

**Check SP:** Spell words from the word list correctly.

# INDEPENDENT WORK

**D** Add <u>s</u> or <u>es</u> to make plural words.

1. boss
2. match
3. rash
4. cone
5. grape
6. room
7. crunch
8. pass

**END OF LESSON 24**

54  Lesson 24

**Name** _____

**25**

**A** Underline each subject. If the subject is a pronoun, write the letter **P** above it.

1. Donald planted corn.

2. It had a broken handle.

3. He kicked a football.

4. Betty is baking a pie.

5. The red truck has 16 wheels.

6. They woke up late.

7. She planted corn.

8. Big bugs are running all over the place.

# INDEPENDENT WORK

**B** Write **V** over the five verbs.

1. paper    2. planted    3. runs    4. rabbit

5. begins   6. biggest    7. sat      8. went

**END OF LESSON 25**

## 26

**A** Underline each subject. If the subject is a pronoun, write the letter **P** above it.

1. The tree is beautiful.
2. He was eating pizza for dinner.
3. Those dogs chased our cat.
4. Tina is reading a book.
5. It fell off the table.
6. They bought new shirts.
7. My sister painted the room.
8. Robert is finishing his homework.

**B** Use the check letters to edit the paragraph.

| | |
|---|---|
| | Roger went inside his tent. He took off |
| **IH** | his boots and went to sleep. The mother gorilla |
| **SP** | took the bananas from the table. She climed |
| **DID** | back up the tree. The baby gorilla waits on |
| **CP** | the branch the mother gorilla gave a banana |
| | to her baby. Roger slept the whole time. |

**END OF LESSON 26**

Name _____

## 27

### A  Underline each subject. If the subject is a pronoun, write the letter P above it.

1. The shirt was dirty.
2. They painted the door.
3. He is ten years old.
4. A new girl came to class.
5. It had big tires.
6. A boy and his friend went to the store.
7. My little brother is seven years old.
8. She walked to school.

### B  Fix the mistakes.

1. They said we are hungry.  (4)
2. She teached jerry to cook.  (2)
3. I said "are you tired?  (3)
4. The bus went up the hill it made lots of noise.  (2)

# INDEPENDENT WORK

### C  Add s or es to make words that tell about more than one.

1. mass
2. block
3. arrow
4. ax
5. kiss
6. beach
7. march
8. bike

**END OF LESSON 27**

## 28   Name _____

**A** Write a comma in each sentence that needs one. Then, circle each subject and underline the whole predicate.

1. The boys went home after school.

2. During the rainstorm our dog howled loudly.

3. After we fixed the car we made dinner.

4. In the morning Jane walked to school.

5. That girl was happy when she got her glasses.

6. He fell asleep while he read a book.

7. After James sat down the music started.

**B** Write the correct end mark for each sentence.

1. When did you go home
2. You can go to the movies
3. Did you find your hat
4. My brother is sick

5. That dog is mean
6. Can you come with us
7. Is your dog in the house

**C** Label each part of speech that is underlined.

1. <u>They</u> <u>went</u> with us.

2. <u>He</u> <u>is</u> <u>sitting</u> with us.

3. <u>She</u> <u>hid</u> inside the barn.

4. She <u>was</u> <u>looking</u> at <u>it</u>.

**D** Use the check letters to edit the paragraph.

| | |
|---|---|
| **IH** | Mrs. Brown put her key in the lock. She |
| **DID CP** | went inside. She leaves her key in the door |
| **CP** | She hung up her coat. she walked back |
| | to the door. |

**Check IH:** Tell the important things that happened in the middle picture.

**Check S:** Write all your sentences correctly (**CP, SP, DID**).

Lesson 28

# INDEPENDENT WORK

**E** Add s or es to make words that tell about more than one.

1. lunch
2. ocean
3. egg
4. grass
5. brush
6. watch
7. ash
8. dog

**F** Capitalize the names in these sentences.

1. Wendy called her aunt marie on the phone.

2. My brother trevor goes to santa vista high school.

3. Jeff's neighbor on juniper street is ruth garcia.

4. Mr. jasper said president lincoln is a famous historical man.

5. Our class read *charlotte's web*.

END OF LESSON 28

Name _____

**A** Label each part of speech that is underlined.

1. They were looking at her.

2. A mouse ran out and scared her.

3. The wolf jumped out of the bushes.

4. It was very soft.

5. A brown dog is following them.

6. She went with him.

**B** Write the correct end mark for each sentence.

1. Where is Tom
2. Tom and Sally went home
3. Did you see that bird
4. Can he eat that big hamburger
5. A bird flew into the room
6. Is your brother here
7. She did not see her friend

END OF LESSON 29

# 30    Name _____

**A**  Write <u>asked</u> or <u>said</u> in each sentence. Then add the end mark.

1. The girl _____, "Will you go with us ___"

2. The girl _____, "I want to go with you ___"

3. My friend _____, "I love baseball ___"

4. My friend _____, "Do you like baseball ___"

5. Ken _____, "Is it snowing ___"

6. Ken _____, "The snow is two feet deep ___"

**B**  Write a comma in each sentence that needs one. Then circle each subject and underline the whole predicate.

1. A cat jumped up when the alarm clock rang.

2. When we got home the dog started barking.

3. In the morning we ate breakfast.

4. While the baby slept we talked quietly.

5. Her brother was happy when he got the letter.

6. They finished the job just before midnight.

7. Before the cooks made lunch they washed their hands.

## C  Fix the mistakes.

1. James said, Today is my birthday. We are having a party. (2)

2. Bill met Alice in the park. She said you look good. (4)

3. Anns dad is very tall he plays basketball. (3)

4. The doctor said you have a bad cold. Don't go outside. (4)

5. I seen ann and jane at Mr. jordans house. (5)

## D  Use the check letters to edit the paragraph.

| | |
|---|---|
| CP | Mr. Jones took a picture of Ann. he |
| SP | got down on one knee. She waved and smild. |
| IH DID | ^ Mr. Jones dropped his camera. He jumps |
| DID | into the pool. He swimmed over to Ann and |
| | grabbed her. |

# INDEPENDENT WORK

## E  Add s or es to make words that tell about more than one.

1. marsh
2. swing
3. switch
4. dish
5. call
6. blush
7. loss
8. walk

**END OF LESSON 30**

## 31  Name _____

### A  For each sentence, write **asked** or **said**. Then make the correct end mark.

1. He _____ , "Why are you so sad ___"

2. She _____ , "He has my book ___"

3. His friend _____ , "Where is the game ___"

4. My sister _____ , "Can we have a cookie ___"

### B  Write each plural word.

1. loaf            2. shelf            3. wolf

   _____       _____          _____

### C  Label each part of speech that is underlined.

1. <u>It</u> <u>was</u> <u>landing</u> on the runway.

2. <u>They</u> wheeled <u>it</u> into the store.

3. The dog <u>barked</u> loudly at <u>him</u>.

4. <u>He</u> <u>forgot</u> his homework.

5. They see <u>it</u> all around <u>them</u>.

6. The students <u>are</u> <u>working</u> for <u>her</u>.

**END OF LESSON 31**

Lesson 31

Name _____

**A** For each sentence, write <u>asked</u> or <u>said</u>. Then make the correct end mark.

1. He _____ , "Is your brother home ___"

2. He _____ , "We had a good time ___"

3. She _____ , "My friend went home ___"

4. She _____ , "Where is the dog ___"

**B** Write each plural word.

1. lunch       2. loaf       3. brush
   _____       _____       _____

4. sister      5. beach      6. grass
   _____       _____       _____

**C** Write each plural word.

1. wolf        2. splash     3. bank
   _____       _____       _____

4. wish        5. shelf      6. catch
   _____       _____       _____

**D** Use the check letters to edit the paragraph.

| | |
|---|---|
| **SP** | Tina had a problim. She was at the parade |
| **CP DID** | but she couldn't see anything there are too |
| **IH** | many people in front of her. ∧ The balloon man |
| | gave her 8 balloons. Tina gave her boots and |
| **IH CP** | coat to her mom. ∧ Tina floated up into the air |
| | Now she could see everything. |

**Check IH:** Tell the important things that happened in the first picture and the middle picture.

**Check S:** Write all your sentences correctly (**CP, SP, DID**).

END OF LESSON 32

66    Lesson 32

Name _____

**33**

**A** Write each plural word.

1. life  2. dish  3. book  4. loaf
_____ _____ _____ _____

5. bench  6. hiss  7. knife  8. box
_____ _____ _____ _____

**B** Label each part of speech that is underlined.

1. The silver wolf <u>jumped</u> out of the bushes.

2. <u>It</u> was very soft.

3. <u>She</u> <u>is</u> with him.

4. They <u>are</u> <u>looking</u> at <u>her</u>.

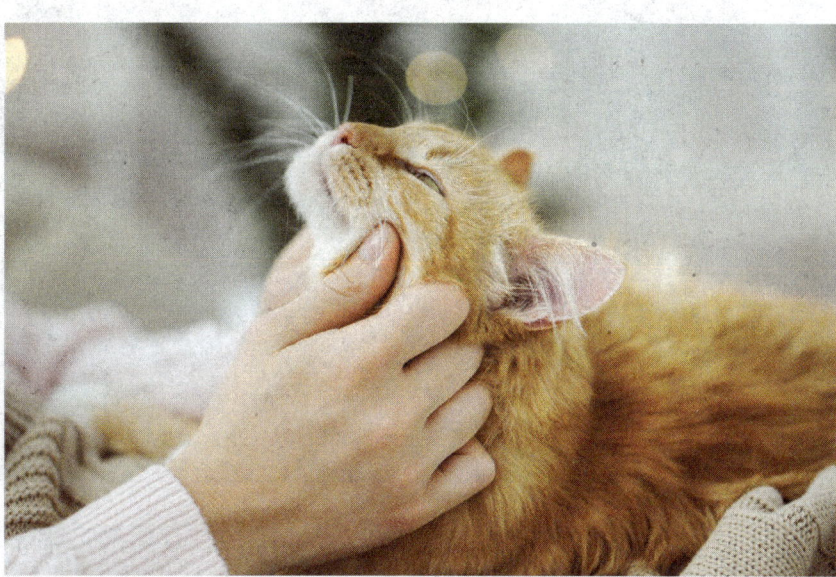

END OF LESSON 33

**34** Name _____

**A** Fix the mistakes in each sentence.

1. At midnight. The dog began to bark.  (2)

2. The streets flooded, during the rainstorm  (2)

3. She bought a book. Before the store closed.  (2)

4. While the wind blew. Everybody stayed inside.  (2)

5. Ann fell asleep while toms dad sang.  (2)

6. Two old trees fell down, last night.  (1)

7. Before Anns dad made breakfast we washed our hands.  (2)

68   Lesson 34

## B  Use the check letters to edit the paragraph.

| | |
|---|---|
| | Jerry's friends had a big lunch at Jerry's |
| **CP** | house They left at 1 o'clock. The kitchen was a |
| | mess. Jerry's mom opened the kitchen door and |
| | said, "Please clean the kitchen while I go |
| **Q** | shopping. She went to the grocery store. Jerry |
| **CP** | worked hard while she was gone he carried the |
| | dirty dishes from the table to the sink. |
| **IH** | He cleaned the table. He mopped the floor. He |
| **SP** | took out the garbidge. He finished cleaning at |
| | 3 o'clock. |

**Check Q:** Correctly punctuate the sentence that tells what somebody said.

# INDENDENT WORK

**C** Label each underlined verb or pronoun.

1. Billy <u>is eating</u> <u>it</u>.
2. The wind <u>is blowing</u> <u>them</u> down.
3. <u>It</u> <u>was moving</u> too fast.
4. A big wind <u>knocked</u> <u>him</u> down.
5. <u>He</u> <u>saw</u> <u>them</u>.
6. Bill <u>was eating</u> lunch.

**D** Rewrite each sentence so it starts with the part that tells when.

1. Our family always visits my grandmother in the winter time.

   _____

   _____

2. We had a long ride home after the ball game.

   _____

   _____

3. They heard a loud noise in the middle of the night.

   _____

   _____

**END OF LESSON 34**

Name _____

**A** Write the correct plural word for each sentence.

1. One goose was old but all the other _____ were young.

   goose   geese   gooses

2. The _____ were hungry.

   wolfs   wolf   wolves

3. She put six _____ on the table.

   glasses   glass   glassz

4. Ginger's front _____ were missing.

   teeth   tooths   tooth

5. He caught a snake that was ten _____ long.

   foots   foot   feet

6. They kept their _____ in a dry place.

   match   matchs   matches

Lesson 35   71

**B** Punctuate the sentences that tell the exact words a person said. Put in the missing commas, quote marks, and capital letters.

Jerry called Tom on the phone. Jerry asked Tom can you go to the movies?

Tom asked his mother can I go to the movies?

His mother said you can go when you finish your homework.

Tom finished his homework quickly. Tom's mom took Jerry and Tom to the movies later that day.

# INDEPENDENT WORK

**C** Capitalize the names in these sentences.

1. Mr. robinson likes to talk about babe ruth and the new york yankees.

2. Jesse went to his uncle jim's house for new year's.

3. The thompson family visited the hollywood museum in los angeles.

4. Yesterday we had ice cream at pip's parlor for lee jackson's birthday.

**END OF LESSON 35**

**Name** _____

## A   Label the noun in each subject with the letter N.

1. Dark clouds covered the sky.

2. An old dog slept on the floor.

3. The trucks got dirty.

4. Her little bike cost a lot of money.

5. My sister walked to school.

## B   Fix the mistakes in each item.

1. When alice got to school. Nobody was there.  (3)

2. Jerry asked his mother can I stay home?"  (3)

3. Tom asked his sister where is my shirt  (5)

4. My sister wasn't home. She went to alices house.  (2)

5. As mr. jordan left. The children waved to him.  (4)

6. Bill cleaned his room, before he ate breakfast  (2)

**C** Use the check letters to edit the paragraph.

|      | |
|------|---|
|      | The sheriff took a shower at the end of a |
| CP   | hard day a deputy came into the shower room. |
| Q    | The deputy said, "We have an emergency call. |
|      | The sheriff got ready as fast as he could. He |
| IH   | hurried out of the shower and grabbed a towel. ∧ |
| SP   | He picked up the emergincy tool kit and ran |
|      | outside in his bare feet. He ran toward the |
| SP   | polece car. His deputy put a leash on the dog. |
|      | He also grabbed the sheriff's shoes and socks. |
| DID  | The deputy and the dog run after the sheriff. |

**Check Q:** Correctly punctuate the sentence that tells what somebody said.

**D** Write the correct nouns below each pronoun.

Nouns:  Mr. Jones   Jane   car   girl   city
man   coat   grandmother   street   boy

| she | he | it |
|---|---|---|
|  |  |  |

# INDEPENDENT WORK

**E** Rewrite each sentence so it starts with the part that tells when.

1. We will go to Spain in February.
   _____

2. My dad likes to go fishing every weekend.
   _____

3. Sara will get home after Joe goes to work.
   _____

**END OF LESSON 36**

**A** Write the correct nouns below each pronoun.

girl    truck    Tom    farm
sister    uncle    Linda    light    boy

| it | her | him |
|---|---|---|
| | | |

**B** Label the pronoun or noun in the subject of each sentence.

1. He fell asleep on the floor.

2. A big bird flew into the nest.

3. Alice came home early.

4. It made a big noise.

5. The young man started to speak.

6. Those girls are my sisters.

**C** **Complete each item.**

Here are short parts that tell when:  At last, Suddenly, Next, Now .

If you write one of these parts at the beginning of a sentence, put a comma after the part.

1. Rita saved money for a year. _____ she had enough money to buy a bike.

2. First, Tom got a paint brush. _____ he got a can of paint.

3. The car was going down the street. _____ it made a great noise and stopped.

4. Tina put on her hat and coat. _____ she was ready to go outside.

**END OF LESSON 37**

## A   Label the pronoun or noun in the subject of each sentence.

1. A broken bottle was on the floor.

2. It cost too much.

3. She is older than her sister.

4. That invention was very helpful.

5. Frogs make funny noises.

6. They are sleeping.

## B   Write each plural word.

1. woman _____

2. goose _____

3. child _____

4. tooth _____

5. mouse _____

6. man _____

7. foot _____

**C** Circle the subject in each sentence. Then underline the whole predicate.

1. Ted and Hilda were on the bank of a stream.

2. When the sun came up, Ginger and Tom walked to the barn.

3. Before school, the little boy looked for them.

4. She felt tired after the party.

**D** Label each underlined part of speech. Use the letter V, N, or P.

1. Ted and <u>Hilda</u> <u>were</u> on the <u>bank</u> of a <u>stream</u>.

2. When the <u>sun</u> came up, Ginger and <u>Tom</u> <u>walked</u> to the <u>barn</u>.

3. Before <u>school</u>, the little <u>boy</u> <u>looked</u> for <u>them</u>.

4. <u>She</u> <u>felt</u> tired after the <u>party</u>.

Lesson 38

**E** Use the check letters to edit the paragraph.

|  |  |
|---|---|
|  | Jill had almost finished painting the porch |
| **CP** | rail. her mother came to the door. She said, |
| **Q DID** | "get ready for your piano lesson." Jill finishes |
|  | painting the rail and cleaned up her mess. She |
| **SP** | put the paint brushez in the paint cleaner. She |
|  | put the lid on the paint. She also folded the |
|  | rags. She took off her work boots and went |
| **IH** | inside.˄ She sat on the piano bench with her |
|  | mother. |

**Check Q:** Correctly punctuate the sentence that tells what somebody said.

**END OF LESSON 38**

Name _____

**A** Label each underlined part of speech.

1. Six <u>rabbits</u> <u>played</u> on <u>it</u>.

2. <u>Tom</u> <u>looked</u> at <u>them</u>.

3. <u>They</u> <u>talked</u> to <u>him</u> after lunch.

4. The <u>movie</u> <u>made</u> <u>her</u> laugh.

5. <u>She</u> <u>saw</u> <u>it</u> when she came home.

6. A big <u>dog</u> <u>was</u> with <u>her</u>.

**B** Write each plural word.

1. sheep _____

2. loaf _____

3. mouse _____

4. foot _____

5. deer _____

6. man _____

7. class _____

8. child _____

Lesson 39

**C** Circle the subject in each sentence. Then underline the whole predicate.

1. A dog and a cat were next to her.

2. After the rain stopped, they went to his house.

3. She put apples and oranges in her bag.

4. Yesterday morning, their mother drove them to school.

**D** Label each underlined part of speech.

1. A <u>dog</u> and a <u>cat</u> <u>were</u> next to <u>her</u>.

2. After the <u>rain</u> <u>stopped</u>, <u>they</u> went to his <u>house</u>.

3. <u>She</u> <u>put</u> <u>apples</u> and <u>oranges</u> in her bag.

4. Yesterday <u>morning</u>, their <u>mother</u> <u>drove</u> <u>them</u> to school.

**END OF LESSON 39**

Name _____

## A  Label each underlined part of speech.

1. She stood next to him.

2. That girl gave him a book.

3. James saw her through that window.

4. Our cat played with them.

5. They were on top of it.

## B  Write each plural word.

1. shelf  _____

2. latch  _____

3. tooth  _____

4. woman  _____

5. sheep  _____

6. chair  _____

7. wife  _____

8. goose  _____

Lesson 40

**C** Use the check letters to edit the paragraph.

|      |                                                                 |
|------|-----------------------------------------------------------------|
|      | The back wheel of Alicia's bike was badly                       |
| CP   | bent. Alicia took her bike to a bike repair shop                |
| Q    | the repair man looked at the bent wheel. "He                    |
|      | said Can I help you? I can fix that bike in                     |
| SP   | five minits." He put the bike in a bike rack.                   |
| IH   | ∧Alicia took her book. She sat on a bench and                   |
| DID  | read while she waited. The bike man works for                   |
|      | a long time but could not fix the wheel.                        |

**Check Q:** Correctly punctuate the sentence that tells what somebody said.

84   Lesson 40

**D** Fix the mistakes.

1. Bill asked his mother when will we eat dinner (5)

2. When the dog barked at a cat. The baby woke up. (2)

3. Tom brushed his teeth, after he washed his face (2)

4. Abdul said, "I am hungry. I want an apple (2)

5. The boys cleaned their teachers desk. (1)

6. Where is mr. suzuki (3)

# INDEPENDENT WORK

**E** Write each plural word.

1. foot
2. corner
3. life
4. ridge
5. tooth
6. guard
7. glass
8. slash
9. goose
10. box
11. self
12. witch

**END OF LESSON 40**

## 41 Name _____

### A Complete each sentence with was or were.

1. Those girls _____ happy.

2. Girls and boys _____ hungry.

3. A baby _____ sleepy.

4. Five dogs _____ chasing a cat.

5. Those three books _____ new.

6. My mother _____ next to the car.

7. He _____ at the park.

8. They _____ late for school.

### B Complete each sentence with the correct plural word.

| child | tooth | man | wolf | broom | glass |

1. Five _____ grew thick fur in the winter.

2. Three _____ fell from the table and broke.

3. There were 20 _____ playing in the school yard.

4. He brushed his _____ with a new toothbrush.

5. His father was standing next to the other _____ .

**C** **Put the missing comma in each sentence that begins with a part that tells when.**

As Wendy drove home from work, she thought of the banana pie that was in the refrigerator. Wendy was very hungry because she had not eaten lunch. After she parked her car, she ran into the kitchen and opened the refrigerator. Wendy could not believe her eyes. The refrigerator was empty. The banana pie was gone. Everything was gone. While Wendy was looking at the empty refrigerator, her brother walked into the kitchen. He looked nervous. After a few seconds, he walked up to his sister and said, "I'm sorry. I had some friends over for lunch and we ate all the food. Wait here. I'll be right back." Wendy sat down and waited. After a few minutes, her brother walked into the kitchen. He was carrying a bag filled with groceries. Later, Wendy took a nap. As she slept, her brother cooked dinner. The dessert was a huge banana pie.

**D** **Label each noun with the letter N.**

1. girl ___
2. men ___
3. they ___
4. us ___
5. yellow ___
6. phone ___
7. happy ___
8. me ___
9. mud ___

**END OF LESSON 41**

### A  Complete each sentence with was or were.

1. My father _____ sick.
2. Her older brothers _____ behind the car.
3. They _____ eating dinner.
4. Two horses _____ in the barn.
5. I _____ walking my dog.
6. Their dad _____ eating lunch.
7. My mother and father _____ happy.

### B  Label each noun with the letter N.

1. pen ___
2. us ___
3. flag ___
4. under ___
5. song ___
6. them ___
7. her ___
8. found ___
9. clouds ___
10. school ___
11. puppies ___
12. party ___

### C  Label each underlined part of speech.

1. <u>They</u> <u>were</u> on top of <u>it</u>.
2. A big <u>dog</u> <u>followed</u> <u>them</u> home.
3. <u>She</u> <u>gave</u> <u>him</u> the ball.
4. <u>Jerry</u> <u>was</u> next to <u>her</u>.

**D** **Put the missing comma in each sentence that begins with a part that tells when.**

Mr. Ross took his family out for dinner at a fancy restaurant. They had a very expensive meal. After they finished the meal, the waiter brought them the bill. Mr. Ross reached into his pocket for his wallet. As he reached into his pocket, he realized that he had left his wallet at home. He told the waiter about his problem. The waiter told the boss that Mr. Ross could not pay the bill.

When the boss heard about the problem, she was not happy. The boss and Mr. Ross talked and came up with a solution to the problem. While his family went home to look for the wallet, Mr. Ross had to wash dishes. Mr. Ross put on an apron and began to wash the dishes. By the time his family came back with his wallet, Mr. Ross had washed all the dishes in the restaurant.

**E** **Complete each sentence with the correct plural.**

| foot   shelf   watch   birthday   shoe |

1. He polished his _____ .
2. Jon knew the correct time because he had two good _____ .
3. There were more than 40 _____ in her library.
4. Wipe your _____ before coming in the house.

**END OF LESSON 42**

# 43   Name _____

## A   Complete each sentence with was or were.

1. Jenny and John _____ reading.

2. That pencil _____ sharp.

3. Five fish _____ swimming in the tank.

4. Terry _____ fishing from the boat.

5. An old woman _____ tired.

6. They _____ playing football.

7. Pedro and I _____ late.

## B   Label each underlined part of speech.

1. She bought a new car.

2. They went to a crowded beach.

3. Sam cooked dinner for them.

4. My truck ran over it.

## C   Complete each sentence with the correct plural word.

class     wish     moon     mouse     fish

1. She liked the teachers in all her _____ .

2. He made three _____ .

3. The _____ ran across the floor.

4. We caught 11 _____ .

**END OF LESSON 43**

Name _____

## A  Complete each sentence with was or were.

1. You _____ right.

2. You _____ late yesterday.

3. She _____ sad.

4. You _____ not home yesterday.

5. He _____ late.

6. They _____ sick.

7. His dog _____ friendly.

8. You _____ hiding.

## B  Write the correct plural word in each blank.

| bench | bird | dish | deer |

1. I don't like to wash _____ .

2. The _____ were flying near the trees.

3. Five _____ walked near our tent.

4. The _____ in the park are painted green.

**C** Use the check letters to edit the passage.

|     |     |
| --- | --- |
|     | Dave was working at an auto repair |
| **CP** | shop he was changing a wheel. He told the |
|     | woman he was working with, "After work, I am |
| **NP** | going to the beach to cool off." When Dave |
|     | finished work, he rode to the beach on his bike. |
|     | His dog ran next to the bike. When he got to |
|     | the beach, Dave changed into his swimsuit. He |
|     | put his uniform and shoes next to his bike. He |
|     | took the leash off his dog and ran through the |
| **DID** | sand into the water. His dog follow him. They |
|     | went swimming. As Dave and his dog ran out of |
|     | the water, Dave said, "I love to go swimming on |
| **Q** | a hot day. |

**D** Label each underlined part of speech.

1. The <u>wind</u> <u>blew</u> <u>water</u> at <u>me</u>.

2. My <u>brother</u> <u>put</u> <u>salt</u> on <u>it</u>.

3. <u>She</u> <u>wanted</u> a new <u>bike</u> last <u>summer</u>.

4. That old <u>man</u> <u>sold</u> <u>it</u> to <u>me</u>.

# INDEPENDENT WORK

**E** Circle the subject and underline the predicate.

1. My favorite uncle is coming to visit next week.

2. The old black cat sleeps a lot.

3. Those girls worked hard yesterday.

**END OF LESSON 44**

## 45 Name _____

**A** Label each underlined part of speech.

1. Tim and Donna were mad at them.

2. He threw it at the wall.

3. The dogs and cats ran after me.

4. Her arm had a bug on it.

# INDEPENDENT WORK

**B** Complete each sentence with was or were.

1. He _____ thinking about something.

2. When you _____ young, you were already busy.

3. They _____ too quiet.

4. His uncle _____ rich.

5. The chair looked good but _____ not comfortable.

6. Those roses _____ beautiful when he picked them.

**END OF LESSON 45**

# 46

Name _____

## A  Complete each item with the word jump or jumps.

1. It _____ .
2. I _____ .
3. We _____ .
4. You _____ .
5. She _____ .
6. He _____ .
7. They _____ .

## B  Label each underlined noun, pronoun, or verb.

1. A <u>girl</u> and her <u>dog</u> <u>chased</u> <u>it</u> around the park.

2. <u>He</u> <u>was</u> between a little <u>desk</u> and a big <u>table</u>.

3. In the <u>morning</u>, <u>she</u> <u>took</u> him to see <u>me</u>.

4. Yesterday morning, <u>they</u> <u>ate</u> <u>eggs</u> and toast for <u>breakfast</u>.

Lesson 46

**C** Fix the passage so that it meets all the checks.

Tracy and Maria were riding their snowmobile near a frozen lake. Nobody lived

**CP** near this lake the snowmobile hit a large rock

**SP** that was covered with snow. The snowmobeel was damaged and couldn't run. Maria said, "We'll

**NP** freeze unless we get out of the cold." The women decided to build an igloo. They took the tool

**IH** kit from the snowmobile. ʌ They stacked up the blocks of ice to make an igloo. When they were finished, it was snowing. As Tracy started to

**Q** crawl inside the igloo, Maria said, "now we'll be a lot warmer."

**END OF LESSON 46**

Name _____

**A** If a subject can be replaced with He, She, or It, circle the correct pronoun. Then write jumps or jump in the blank.

1. The girl _____ .  He  She  It

2. You and I _____ .  He  She  It

3. The men _____ .  He  She  It

4. Those frogs _____ .  He  She  It

5. Henry _____ .  He  She  It

6. Mark and Henry _____ .  He  She  It

7. The flea _____ .  He  She  It

**B** Write the letters of all the pictures that each description could tell about.

A.    B.    C.    D.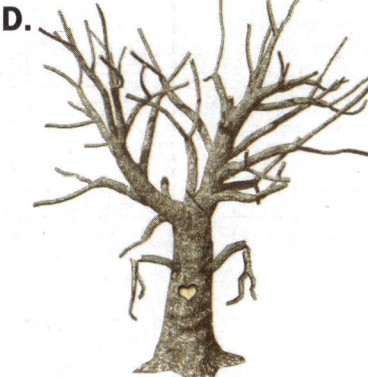

1. The tree was small. _____

2. The tree was small. It had broken branches. _____

3. The tree was small. It had broken branches. It had a heart carved on it. _____

**END OF LESSON 47**

Lesson 47   97

# 48

**A** Fix the passage so that it meets all the checks.

|  |  |
|---|---|
|  | Tony and Rita were driving in their truck. |
|  | They came to a tunnel. The truck was too tall |
| CP | to get through the tunnel Tony and Rita got out |
| DID | of the truck. Tony looks at the tunnel. He |
| SP | asked, "How can we get throogh this tunnel?" |
|  | Rita looked at the front tire. |
|  | Rita got an idea. They could let some air |
|  | out of the tires to make the truck lower. They |
|  | let air out of all the tires. Finally, they drove |
| CP | slowly through the tunnel the truck was low |
| IH | enough to get through safely.^ |

**B** If a subject can be replaced with **He**, **She**, or **It**, circle the correct pronoun. Then write **run** or **runs** in the blank.

1. The woman _____ .  He   She   It

2. Boys and girls _____ .  He   She   It

3. Linda _____ .  He   She   It

4. Her brothers _____ .  He   She   It

5. Her brother _____ .  He   She   It

6. The old car _____ .  He   She   It

7. Two men _____ .  He   She   It

# INDEPENDENT WORK

**C** Complete each sentence with **was** or **were**.

1. The phone _____ not working.

2. Our ideas _____ interesting.

3. How old _____ you when you started school?

4. The oldest of the brothers _____ named Horace.

5. Not all the people _____ happy that evening.

Lesson 48

**D** Label each underlined noun, pronoun, or verb.

1. My uncle walks his dog every day.

2. You were with them last summer.

3. Jane saw me in the mirror when I arrived.

4. We flew 500 miles to see her.

**E** Write the correct plural word in each blank.

| wife | child | glass | bone | fish | box | goose |

1. How many _____ are in your aquarium?

2. The farm had goats, chickens, and _____ .

3. Walter could see better with his new _____ .

4. There are 25 _____ in our class.

5. The meeting was for fishermen and their _____ .

6. We packed our things in big bags and _____ .

**END OF LESSON 48**

Name _____

**A** Punctuate each sentence correctly.

1. The tank held fish snakes frogs and rocks.

2. James read a book wrote two letters called his uncle and cleaned his room.

3. A cat a dog a pig and a horse ran into the barn.

4. They ate burgers salad and cherries for lunch.

**B** Rewrite 3 sentences so they begin with the part that tells when.

Roger took off his boots and lay down on his cot. [1]The mother gorilla came down from the tree after Roger went to sleep. She took the bananas from the table. [2]The baby gorilla was happy when her mother came back. The mother gorilla gave a banana to her baby. [3]Roger stayed asleep while they ate the bananas.

**END OF LESSON 49**

## 50   Name _____

**A**   Punctuate each sentence correctly.

1. Tom ate chicken peas tomatoes and carrots.

2. Jane jumped rope climbed on the bars and walked on her hands.

3. Jerry screamed jumped up and ran to the door.

4. A book a pencil a cup and a spoon fell off the table.

5. Alice opened the door got into the car and drove to work.

6. James his mom and his sister went home.

7. Jane Tom Sarah and Bill ate lunch under the tree.

**B**   If a subject can be replaced with **He**, **She**, or **It**, circle the correct pronoun. Then write **hop** or **hops** in each blank.

1. Joan and Barry _____ over logs.        He    She    It

2. Maria _____ over logs.        He    She    It

3. His dad and her mom _____ over logs.        He    She    It

4. This thin man _____ over logs.        He    She    It

5. The rabbit _____ over logs.        He    She    It

6. I _____ over logs.        He    She    It

**C** Fix the paragraph so that it meets the check.

|     |     |
| --- | --- |
|     | Roger was studying plants in the jungle. |
| COM | After he got back to his campsite he was hungry. He made soup for supper. Two gorillas watched him while he ate a banana. Roger said, "I'm tired. I need to rest." |
|     | Roger took off his boots and lay down on his cot. The mother gorilla climbed down the tree when Roger went to sleep. The baby gorilla waited on the branch. Her mother came back after grabbing the bananas. Roger snored loudly while the happy gorillas ate the bananas. |
| W   |     |

**Check W:** Write at least 2 sentences that begin with a part that tells when (W, COM).

**END OF LESSON 50**

# 51

**A** Circle the correct word for each item.

1. Milly played baseball with Linda. **Milly / She** threw the ball.

2. Milly played baseball with Jeff. **Milly / She** threw the ball.

3. Gary and John went to the store. **John / He** had been working all day.

4. Jessica talked to Liz. **Jessica / She** was walking home.

5. Kathy handed a glass to Bill. **Kathy / She** told him where to put it.

**B** Punctuate each sentence correctly.

1. Jerry got into the car turned on the engine and drove home.

2. Mary Jim and Tom were sick yesterday.

3. James ate a piece of bread and drank a glass of milk.

4. Bill wore black shoes a red shirt and brown pants.

5. A cat a dog a goat and a pig lived in the barn.

6. My mother and my little sister walked to the store.

7. Walter washed the windows made his bed and swept the floor.

**END OF LESSON 51**

Name _____

## 52

### A  Punctuate each sentence correctly.

1. They bought three apples and six oranges.

2. His sister bought five apples two oranges and three carrots.

3. Raymond and Ned talked quietly.

4. Alice Julio Brandi and Clark talked quietly.

5. We cleaned our room ate dinner and did our homework before we went to sleep.

### B  If a subject can be replaced with He, She, or It, circle the pronoun. Then write sing or sings in each blank.

1. His dad _____ well.                He    She    It

2. His dad and mom _____ well.       He    She    It

3. You _____ well.                    He    She    It

4. Those ten kids _____ well.         He    She    It

5. The young girl _____ well.         He    She    It

6. Her older brothers _____ well.     He    She    It

7. The yellow canary _____ well.      He    She    It

Lesson 52   105

**C** Fix the paragraph so that it meets the checks.

|  |  |
|---|---|
|  | Jerry and his friends finished eating lunch |
|  | at 1 o'clock. The kitchen was a mess. As Jerry's |
| COM | friends were leaving Jerry's mom opened the |
|  | kitchen door. She said, "Please clean up this |
| NP | mess." Jerry worked hard while his mom went |
|  | shopping for groceries. He carried the dirty |
|  | dishes from the table to the sink. He cleaned |
| DID | the table. He washes all the dishes and puts |
|  | them away. He took out the garbage after he |
|  | mopped the floor. His mom walked into the room |
|  | just as he finished cleaning. Jerry said, |
|  | "Everything is cleaned up. What's for dinner?" |
| W |  |

**Check W:** Write at least 2 sentences that begin with a part that tells when (W, COM).

**END OF LESSON 52**

Name _____

**A** Circle the correct word for each item.

1. Tom waved to Martha. Martha / She was riding a horse.

2. Larry wanted to meet James. Larry / He had a new bike.

3. Barbara gave her sister a rabbit. Her sister / She loved rabbits.

4. Mr. Ross and Mr. Long were teachers. Mr. Ross / He taught math.

5. Linda went fishing with Bill. Bill / He caught four fish.

6. Ann and Sandra went to a party. Ann / She carried a cake.

# INDEPENDENT WORK

**B** Complete each sentence with was or were.

1. My uncle _____ earlier than usual.

2. You _____ always kind to me.

3. Our parents _____ happy to see us.

4. My cat _____ missing for two days.

5. They _____ late for the bus.

**END OF LESSON 53**

Lesson 53

# 54  Name _____

## A  Circle the correct word for each item.

1. Wendy and Debbie went to the beach.  Wendy / She  flew her kite.

2. Robert and Dave walked home.  Dave / He  carried a radio.

3. Tom and Pam walked to school.  Tom / He  liked to walk fast.

4. Ed and Sam talked in the hall.  Ed / He  stood near the door.

5. Linda helped Alice build a table.  Linda / She  wanted to paint it red.

6. Alice asked Bob about school.  Alice / She  had been absent for a week.

## B  Write **talk** or **talks** in each blank.

1. That man _____ fast.

2. She _____ fast.

3. I _____ fast.

4. Alvin and his brother _____ fast.

5. Six parrots _____ fast.

6. It _____ fast.

Lesson 54

**C** Fix the passage so that it meets the checks.

|     |     |
| --- | --- |
|     | Dan and Oliver decided to go fishing. They set their alarm clock before they went to sleep. |
|     | The boys got up when the alarm clock went off. |
| SP  | They got out of bed, got dressed, and went outside. They put the boat on the trailr. |
|     | Dan's dad drove the truck to the lake. |
| COM | When they arrived they put the boat in the water. Both boys put on their life jackets. Oliver took the oars and sat in the front seat. Dan sat in the back with the fishing pole. Oliver rowed |
| Q   | to the middle of the lake. He said "we're going to be lucky today. I bet we catch ten fish." |
| W   |     |

**Check W:** Write at least 2 sentences that begin with a part that tells when (W, COM).

**END OF LESSON 54**

## 55

**A** Circle the correct word for each item.

1. Bill and Frank ate lunch. **Bill / He** had a peanut butter sandwich.

2. Miss Winston and Miss Kelly were teachers. **Miss Kelly / She** taught reading.

3. Kevin told Ann about a movie. **Kevin / He** thought it was very funny.

4. My father gave Betty a book. **Betty / She** liked to read books about space.

5. Tina sat next to Jane. **Tina / She** was the smartest girl in the class.

6. Wendy worked with Bill. **Wendy / She** fixed a flat tire.

**B** Write **run** or **runs** in each blank.

1. Those cars _____ on batteries.

2. Dogs _____ faster than people.

3. It _____ at the racetrack.

4. My mother _____ a marathon every year.

5. You _____ like the wind.

6. This thin man _____ four miles every day.

## C  Fix the mistakes in each item.

1. Tom and I was both born on the first wednesday in december. (3)

2. Janes hands got dirty, when she planted trees (3)

3. Ann visited her grandmother every monday night in april and may. (3)

4. Cats and dogs was running in Toms yard. (2)

5. Alex and i were talking to cora. (2)

6. Kay asked her dad  can i stay up late? (5)

7. When mr. adams got home on Thursday. He read the newspaper. (4)

**END OF LESSON 55**

## 56 Name _____

### A  Fill in the blanks.

_____ and _____ were swimming. _____ wore a bathing cap. _____ also wore a watch. _____ sat near the water. _____ wore sunglasses. _____ stood next to the blanket. _____ wore shorts. _____ read a book.

# INDEPENDENT WORK

### B  Complete each sentence with like or likes.

1. His dad _____ golf.

2. His grandparents _____ to dance.

3. Kittens _____ milk.

4. Our teacher _____ to play piano.

5. She _____ to ride a bike.

6. We _____ swimming lessons.

**END OF LESSON 56**

**Name** _____

**57**

**A** Fill in the blanks.

_____ and _____ picked apples from a tree. _____ wore a hat. _____ had a beard. _____ stood on a box. _____ held a bucket. _____ and _____ sat on a blanket. _____ read a book. _____ wore a shirt with the number 9 on the back. _____ drew a picture.

# INDEPENDENT WORK

**B** Punctuate sentences that need commas.

1. Janice had a cat two goldfish and a dog.
2. Mr. James took Al Cindy Yetta and Francine to the park.
3. Our friend and her mother came over to listen to music.
4. The mouse found a dime an old cap a button and a red stone.
5. The knives forks and spoons were in the top drawer.

**END OF LESSON 57**

# 58

**Name** _____

**A** Fill in the blanks.

_____ and _____ were playing basketball.

_____ dribbled a ball. _____ wore shorts and long

socks. _____ wore a headband to keep her hair from getting in

her eyes. _____ jumped into the air as she shot the ball toward

the basket. _____ leaned against a pole as she watched

the girls play basketball. _____ read a newspaper.

_____ sat on a bench.

# INDEPENDENT WORK

**B** Complete each sentence with <u>feel</u> or <u>feels</u>.

1. She _____ sick.

2. My feet _____ sore.

3. These slippers _____ like silk.

4. We _____ angry about the test.

5. This bed _____ too hard.

6. They _____ shy about singing.

7. His forehead _____ hot.

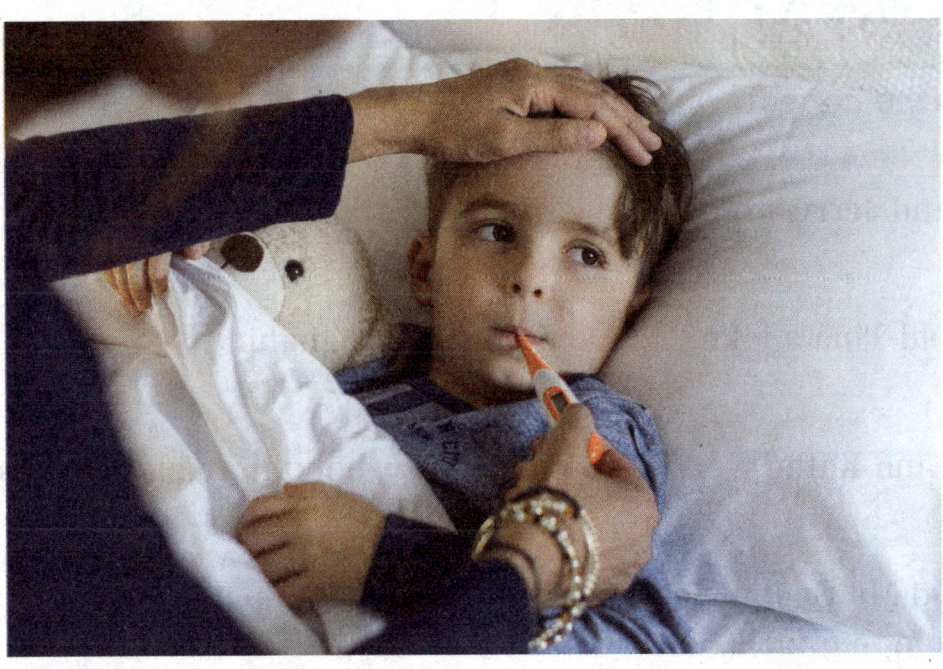

**END OF LESSON 58**

# 59 Name _____

**A** Circle the correct word for each item.

1. Ann walked to school with Jenny. A car splashed water on Ann. / her.

2. Randy and Steve ran down the street. A black cat ran in front of Steve. / him.

3. Tom saw Nancy at the store. The clerk was giving Nancy / her change.

4. Frank was talking to Peter. Everybody liked Peter. / him.

5. Beth went swimming with Mike. She splashed water at Mike. / him.

## INDEPENDENT WORK

**B** Circle the correct word for each item.

1. Burt and Jerry were in the garage. Jerry / He was trying to fix his bike.

2. Ben told Tina a joke. Tina / She couldn't stop laughing.

3. Linda and Kathy went shopping. Linda / She bought a yellow dress.

4. Bill and Mr. Smith spent a week working on a path. Mr. Smith / He had very good digging tools.

5. Maria and Ted were in the school play. Ted / He had the main role.

**END OF LESSON 59**

# 60

**Name** _____

## A  Circle the correct word for each item.

1. Don and Mark raked leaves. Carol gave [Don / him] a bag for the leaves.

2. Mr. Swift fixed lunch for Miss Adams. He gave [Miss Adams / her] a large bowl of soup.

3. Linda wanted to be a clown for Halloween. Steve found a funny outfit for [Linda / her] to wear.

4. Tina and Alice waited in the doctor's office. The nurse told [Alice / her] to go into another room.

5. Jeff and Kurt left school. Mr. Dukes gave [Kurt / him] a ride home.

## B  Fix the mistakes in each sentence.

1. Mr. Adams and mrs. sanchez was sick on wednesday.  (4)

2. Jill asked Tom can i help you?"  (4)

3. When my mom walked into the room. My baby sister smiled.  (2)

4. Where did you put Jills coat  (2)

5. You was born in february.  (2)

6. She asked was he born in april or may?"  (5)

Lesson 60   117

**C** Make an outline.

1. **clothing**
   a. _____
   b. _____
   c. _____

2. **tools**
   a. _____
   b. _____
   c. _____

3. **vehicles**
   a. _____
   b. _____
   c. _____

# INDEPENDENT WORK

**D** Complete each sentence with **help** or **helps**.

1. Sasha _____ her little sister tie her shoes.

2. They sometimes _____ in the garden.

3. Nassir _____ his dad clean the garage.

4. She _____ her group learn math facts.

5. The parents _____ keep score of the game.

6. My big brother _____ bag the groceries.

7. I _____ my mom do the dishes every day.

**END OF LESSON 60**

# 61

Name _____

## A  Make an outline.

1. Fruits          2. Vegetables          3. Animals

___ _____     ___ _____        ___ _____

___ _____     ___ _____        ___ _____

___ _____     ___ _____        ___ _____

___ _____     ___ _____        ___ _____

## B  Circle the correct word to complete each item.

1. The dogs chased the cats. I watched ( the cats / them ) climb up a tree.

2. The boys and girls cleaned the house. ( The boys / They ) washed the windows.

3. The rabbits ran under the fence. ( The rabbits / They ) wanted the carrots.

4. Linda spoke to the boys. She told ( the boys / them ) about the test.

5. He washed the forks and spoons. He put ( the forks / them ) on the table.

**END OF LESSON 61**

## 62  Name _____

**A** Circle the correct words to complete the items.

1. Sally had pencils and pens. She gave [the pens / them] to her friend.

2. Tony found two kittens. He gave [the kittens / them] some milk.

3. We saw bears and elephants. [The elephants / They] were eating peanuts.

4. The boys and girls played baseball. [The girls / They] won the game.

5. The birds flew into the barn. [The birds / They] stayed in the barn all night.

# INDEPENDENT WORK

**B** Write **climb** or **climbs** in each blank.

1. Her little sister _____ over the garden gate.

2. She _____ into her bed.

3. The athletes _____ the rock walls.

4. He _____ the rope in gym class.

5. The ivy _____ the forest trees.

6. Tom and Jamie _____ over the logs in the stream.

7. You _____ to the top of the hill and tell us what you see.

**END OF LESSON 62**

Name _____

**A** Make an outline.

# Things I Did

1. _____  2. _____  3. _____

___. _____

   a. _____
   b. _____
   c. _____
   d. _____

___. _____

   a. _____
   b. _____
   c. _____
   d. _____

___. _____

   a. _____
   b. _____
   c. _____
   d. _____

Lesson 63

**B** Fix up the four unclear words in this passage.

One day, Tom went to the park with his dog and a flying disc. The dog loved to play with the disc and wagged its tail as they went to the park. As Tom and his dog played, they came out of the woods to watch.

Tom was pretending he was a star baseball player. He threw the flying disc as hard as he could. It went over the dog's head and landed in the field. Tom and his dog ran after the disc. It chewed on the disc.

As the dog barked at the bear cubs, she came out from behind the trees. When Tom saw the mother bear, he grabbed it and climbed up a tree.

**END OF LESSON 63**

Name _____

**A** Fix up the five unclear words.

Ramon and Kevin worked at a rodeo. Kevin was a cowboy who rode bulls. He was a rodeo clown who helped cowboys.

One day, he tried to ride a fierce bull. He held on tightly as the bull jumped up and down. Suddenly, the bull turned sharply and threw Kevin to the ground. As Kevin sat on the ground holding his leg, he ran into the rodeo arena holding it. Ramon put the barrel down on the ground and began to yell at the bull. The bull turned and ran toward the barrel. While Ramon helped Kevin walk away, it hit the barrel with its horns. Ramon had once again helped a cowboy who was in danger.

**END OF LESSON 64**

# 65

**A** Fix up the three unclear words in this passage.

Raymond loved to throw rocks. While Raymond was walking through the woods one day, he picked up some rocks and started throwing them at a tree. One rock missed the tree and hit it.

They were very mad. They flew out of the hive and headed straight toward Raymond. He ran away as quickly as he could. Just before the bees reached Raymond, he jumped into it. He stayed in the river until the bees returned to their nest.

### B  Fix the mistakes in each sentence.

1. Jerry asked, "can Raymond and i go to the movies  (4)

2. My dads hand is twice as big as Jerrys hand.  (2)

3. When the baby fell asleep. Everybody was happy.  (2)

4. Alice Chuck and ellen ate lunch at Ellens house.  (4)

5. December january and february was cold months.  (5)

6. Alice was very tired, when she got home on monday.  (2)

# INDEPENDENT WORK

### C  Circle the correct word for each item.

1. Martha met her brother at school. Their father drove  Martha / her  there.

2. Sarah gave Ben and Sam presents. She gave  Ben / him  a skateboard.

3. David and Mike went to the pool. I took a sandwich to  Mike / him .

4. Sue and Ian ran a race. Sue could not keep up with  Ryan / him .

**END OF LESSON 65**

# 66  Name _____

**A** Fix up the three unclear words in this passage.

Early one morning, Tina drove her car to the garage where Robert, Sam, and Jane worked. After Tina parked her car in front of the gas pumps, he walked to the back of the car and opened the lid of the gas tank. As Robert put gas in the car, he cleaned the front windshield. She bent down and took a tire off a car while the men worked on Tina's car.

**B** For each sentence, underline the subject. Then label the noun and each adjective in the subject.

1. An old tree grew next to the house.

2. That farmer had big hands.

3. A little black cat ran in front of me.

4. Small clouds moved across the sky.

5. Those happy boys cheered loudly.

6. The dog was hungry.

# INDEPENDENT WORK

**C** Label each underlined noun, pronoun, and verb. Use P, N, and V.

1. He put the clean dishes in the cupboard.

2. They told him to hide in the room when the door slammed.

3. The vest was orange and white with buttons.

4. We cleaned the horse barn for them.

5. Anne walked across the bridge to her.

**END OF LESSON 66**

## 67

**A** For each sentence, underline the subject. Then label the noun and any adjectives in the subject.

1. Our teacher gave books to the children.

2. A man fixed her water pipes.

3. Nine red bugs were on my sandwich.

4. My younger sister fixed our car.

**B** Fix the sentences that tell the exact words that somebody said.

James did not do his homework last night. He said my teacher won't care. She likes me.

James was wrong. His teacher did care. She said you will stay in from recess to finish your work.

James was not happy during recess. He said I will finish my homework tonight. I don't like missing recess.

# INDEPENDENT WORK

### C  Complete each sentence with live or lives.

1. My aunt _____ in Canada.

2. Three bears _____ in the woods.

3. We _____ on the other side of town.

4. My best friend _____ next door.

5. You _____ too far away.

6. Lots of ducks _____ on the lake.

7. A spider _____ under the sink.

### D  Circle the correct word in each item.

1. Maddy and Rita went to the park. Rita / She sat on the blue swing.

2. Pedro and Maria like to swim. Pedro / He goes to the pool every day.

3. My dad and his friend went fishing. My dad / He caught three fish for dinner.

4. Sara and Julia ran a race. Sara / She won!

5. Ryan and his sister were late for school. His sister / She couldn't find her backpack.

**END OF LESSON 67**

## 68

**A** Make the missing quote marks.

> Start a new paragraph each time a different person talks.

James and Janice were talking. James said, "I hate to stay indoors when the days are sunny."

Janice said, "I hate to spend a lot of time in the hot sun."

James looked at her and said, "Well, you can always find a shady spot. You just have to look around."

Janice said, What do you do if you're in a place that does not have any shady spots?

James shrugged and said, I don't know.

Janice said, So it's not true you can always find a shady spot. James didn't know what to say, so he just looked down and didn't say anything.

**B** Underline each subject. Then label the noun and any adjectives in the subject.

1. Seven little bugs were on the table.

2. Her best friend was not at school.

3. Dogs chased the cats.

4. An airplane landed on the runway.

5. Their mother played piano.

6. His blue pants are too tight.

END OF LESSON 68

**A** Label both nouns in each sentence. Then label the adjectives.

1. His brother bought a new hat.

2. My sister baked a yellow cake.

3. Five red ants climbed the wall.

4. An old green cup fell off the big table.

**B** Make the missing quote marks.

David walked up to his sister. He said I have a problem. My bike won't work.

She said I will help you fix it. They worked for two hours. After they finished, the bike worked as well as it ever worked.

David said Thanks a lot. I am really happy that you are my sister.

**C**    **Fix the mistakes in each sentence.**

1. The mississippi river is the longest river in the united states. (4)

2. Texas alaska and california are the biggest states. (4)

3. Is los angeles bigger than san francisco? (4)

4. We lived on baldwin street until last august. (3)

5. After she brushed her teeth. She went to bed. (2)

6. My favorite cities are new york dallas and miami. (6)

7. Ann asked mr. james Where can i buy that book (7)

**END OF LESSON 69**

**A** Label both nouns in each sentence. Then label the adjectives.

1. One man held a big net.

2. Her sons bought ten cookies.

3. The gray squirrel climbed a tall tree.

4. Six children washed three little dogs.

# INDEPENDENT WORK

**B** Punctuate the sentences that tell the exact words that someone said.

Maria's birthday was two weeks away. She asked her mom Can I have a new bike for my birthday?

Her mom replied, a bike costs a lot of money." Is there anything else you would like?"

Maria looked sad. When her birthday arrived, she thought she would get something small. Instead, her mom rolled a brand new bike into her room. Maria said "wow! That is the best gift ever. Thanks mom

END OF LESSON 70

Name _____

**A** Write adjectives to complete each subject.

1. _____ rabbit    3. _____ cup

2. _____ men       4. _____ monster

**B** Label the noun and each adjective.

1. The smallest rabbit        3. A small brown cup

2. Those old men              4. A terrible monster

# INDEPENDENT WORK

**C** Label each underlined word as a noun, pronoun, or verb. Use N, P, or V.

1. We looked through the window and saw a large dog.

2. After Ray washed the dishes, he dried them.

3. They paint houses every weekend.

4. My brother gave her lots of new pencils.

**END OF LESSON 71**

## 72  Name _____

**A** Circle each word that should not be capitalized. Then write the title with the correct words capitalized.

1. Vacation In The Mountains

   _____

2. How To Repair A Flat Tire

   _____

3. Mary, Martha, And Mom

   _____

4. Who Needs A Better Pen?

   _____

5. Journey To The Biggest Planet

   _____

**B** Label each noun and each adjective.

1. Three sad clowns rode a tiny bicycle.

2. Kathy is sleeping on the couch.

3. A striped kite hit the tree.

4. A cow ate grass.

5. Ten plates were broken in the old box.

**END OF LESSON 72**

**A** Circle each word that should not be capitalized. Then write the title with the correct words capitalized.

1. My Visit With A Pilot In The Sky

2. Brian's Box Of Tricks And Treats

3. Living On The Edge Of Life

4. The Smallest Things In The World

5. Who Waters The Cabbage?

END OF LESSON 73

# 74

**A** Circle each word that should <u>not</u> be capitalized. Then write the title with the correct words capitalized.

1. A Busy Day In The Emergency Room

   _____

2. Fran And Her Friends

   _____

3. I Know The Strongest Man In The World

   _____

4. Living With A Fussy Person

   _____

5. Our Father And Mother Went To The Moon

   _____

**B** Label each noun and each adjective.

1. His bear juggled three balls.

2. A sick boy sat in a wheelchair.

3. Al ate two apples.

4. That woman held a small red purse.

5. Three people fixed that old red car.

**C** Fix the mistakes in each sentence.

1. The empire state building is in new york.  (5)

2. Robert fed the dog washed the dishes and cleaned his room before lunch.  (2)

3. Is mexico larger than canada  (3)

4. Jill asked, "Where is Dr. Lees office?  (2)

5. I bought apples oranges and pears at the store.  (2)

6. December january and february are the coldest months of the year.  (4)

7. Yokos sister lives on washington street.  (3)

8. Tom and his sister was in the park.  (1)

END OF LESSON 74

# 75

**A** Write a main-idea sentence for each passage.

Passage 1:

Steve took out some paper and a pen. He wrote on the paper. He put the paper in an envelope. He wrote his grandmother's name and address on the envelope. He put a stamp on the envelope.

_____

Passage 2:

Melody put some paper in the fireplace. She put wood on top of the paper. She lit a match and held it under the paper. When the paper and wood started to burn, Melody closed the screen in front of the fireplace.

_____

# INDEPENDENT WORK

**B** Circle each word that should <u>not</u> be capitalized. Then write the title with the correct words capitalized.

1. Alex And The Goldfish
   _____

2. Trail To The Pond
   _____

3. The Tale Of The Road To Grandma's
   _____

4. Our Last Day At Camp
   _____

5. A Story For Every Child
   _____

**C** Label each underlined word as a noun, pronoun, or verb. Use <u>N</u>, <u>P</u>, or <u>V</u>.

1. Our <u>mother</u> <u>made</u> a tasty <u>cake</u>.

2. When <u>Rita</u> <u>finished</u> her walk, <u>she</u> took a <u>shower</u>.

3. Mike <u>gave</u> <u>me</u> a blue <u>backpack</u>.

4. <u>He</u> always <u>has</u> a big <u>smile</u> on his <u>face</u>.

**END OF LESSON 75**

## 76

**A** Complete each sentence with the word **and** or the word **but**.

- The boys painted the fence, **and** they raked the front yard.
- She worked very hard, **but** she did not earn much money.

1. She was tired, _____ her hands were sore.

2. The car is old, _____ it is in very good shape.

3. Her legs were skinny, _____ she could run fast.

4. They will go on a boat, _____ they will go on a train.

# INDEPENDENT WORK

**B** Label each noun and each adjective.

1. Five yellow flowers were growing in the bucket.

2. Sally ran into a big, beautiful field.

3. A tall man gave me three shiny coins.

4. Some people love to swim in the ocean.

5. My neighbor showed me her best photos.

**END OF LESSON 76**

Name _____

**A** **Complete each sentence with the word <u>and</u> or the word <u>but</u>.**

1. James is very friendly, _____ James doesn't smile much.

2. James is very friendly, _____ James almost never talks.

3. James is very friendly, _____ a lot of people like James.

4. James is very friendly, _____ James likes to be with people.

5. James is very friendly, _____ James gets into many fights.

# INDEPENDENT WORK

**B** **Label each underlined noun, pronoun, and verb. Use <u>N</u>, <u>P</u>, and <u>V</u>.**

1. <u>She</u> <u>used</u> lined <u>paper</u> to write a good <u>story</u>.

2. When <u>Mario</u> <u>went</u> to the doctor's office, <u>he</u> <u>had</u> a <u>fever</u>.

3. The <u>hat</u> <u>was</u> red and blue, with a white <u>ribbon</u>.

4. <u>We</u> <u>watched</u> <u>him</u> <u>jump</u> over the <u>fence</u>.

**END OF LESSON 77**

# 78 Name

**A** Complete each sentence with the word <u>and</u> or the word <u>but</u>.

1. The day was very hot, _____ my brother wore his winter coat.

2. The day was very hot, _____ everybody went swimming.

3. The day was very hot, _____ we could see snow near the road.

4. The day was very hot, _____ we stayed at the beach all day.

5. The day was very hot, _____ nobody wore shorts.

# INDEPENDENT WORK

**B** Label each noun and each adjective.

1. The biggest store has the best prices.

2. Five yellow flowers are growing in this garden.

3. Many people like to fly kites.

4. Rachel lives in the small white house.

**END OF LESSON 78**

Name _____

**A** Complete each sentence with the word <u>and</u> or the word <u>but</u>.

1. Alice loved animals, _____ she spent hours at the zoo.

2. Alice loved animals, _____ she didn't want to own a dog.

3. Alice loved animals, _____ she was afraid of cats.

4. Alice loved animals, _____ she wanted to be an animal doctor.

# INDEPENDENT WORK

**B** Circle the correct main-idea sentence.

Ray and his mom got there at 11 o'clock. Ray's favorite animals are polar bears, so they went to look at them first. After that, they saw lions, monkeys, and camels. After lunch, they saw lots more animals. The penguins made Ray laugh. By 4 o'clock, they were ready to go home.

- The zoo had lots of different animals.
- Ray and his mom spent the day at the zoo.
- Ray loves polar bears.
- Ray and his mom had lunch at the zoo.

**END OF LESSON 79**

### A  Complete each sentence with the word <u>and</u> or the <u>word</u> but.

1. She was very smart, _____ she didn't do well in school.

2. She loved animals, _____ she was always bringing home stray cats.

3. The sun came out, _____ the ice did not melt.

4. The dog was small, _____ it had a loud bark.

5. She worked hard, _____ she got good grades.

6. His brother was sick, _____ he went to school.

## INDEPENDENT WORK

### B  Label each noun and each adjective.

1. Six red balloons flew up into the night sky.

2. Nineteen teachers work in our school.

3. My cousin ran home.

4. The bright sun shone in a clear sky.

5. Philip works in the factory.

**END OF LESSON 80**

Name _____

**A** **Complete each sentence with the word <u>and</u> or the word <u>but</u>.**

1. The alarm clock rang, _____ James got out of bed.

2. Everybody likes that singer, _____ nobody buys her records.

3. His teeth were white and shiny, _____ he had bad breath.

4. They used the phone a lot, _____ they had a big phone bill.

5. The room was very comfortable, _____ it was a terrible color.

**B** **Rewrite each item so it starts with the words <u>According</u> <u>to</u>.**

1. Sonia said, "We should have a longer vacation."
   _____
   _____

2. Dr. Woods wrote, "Roger needs an operation."
   _____
   _____

3. My neighbor stated, "It will be sunny next week."
   _____
   _____

4. Chuck Arthur said, "Blue whales are the largest animals."
   _____
   _____

**END OF LESSON 81**

Lesson 81  147

# 82

**A** Use your notes and the outline to write a passage.

## How Toads Stay Alive

(Two main ways) _____
_____

According to Mrs. Engel, _____
_____
_____

According to Mr. Mann, _____
_____
_____

(Two main ways) _____
_____

**Check M:** Tell the main ideas at the beginning and at the end of the passage.

**Check SP:** Spell all the words from your notes correctly.

**Check O:** Use your own sentences.

**Check P:** Write more than three paragraphs.

**Check S:** Punctuate sentences correctly.

**END OF LESSON 82**

**Name** _____

**A** Use your notes and the outline to write a passage.

# Why Bees Are Important

(Two main reasons) ▬▬▬▬▬▬▬▬▬
▬▬▬▬▬▬▬▬▬▬▬▬▬▬▬▬▬

According to Bernice Barker, ▬▬▬▬▬▬
▬▬▬▬▬▬▬▬▬▬▬▬▬▬▬▬▬
▬▬▬▬▬▬▬▬▬▬▬▬▬▬▬▬▬

According to Melissa Morrow, ▬▬▬▬▬
▬▬▬▬▬▬▬▬▬▬▬▬▬▬▬▬▬
▬▬▬▬▬▬▬▬▬▬▬▬▬▬▬▬▬

(Two main reasons) ▬▬▬▬▬▬▬▬▬
▬▬▬▬▬▬▬▬▬▬▬▬▬▬▬▬▬

**Check M:** Tell the main ideas at the beginning and at the end of the passage.

**Check SP:** Spell all the words from your notes correctly.

**Check O:** Use your own sentences.

**Check P:** Write more than three paragraphs.

**Check S:** Punctuate sentences correctly.

**END OF LESSON 83**

# 84

**A** **Use your notes and the outline to write a passage.**

## Where Would We Be Without Wheels?

(Main Ideas) _____

According to Charles Wood, _____

According to Robert Milo, _____

(My life without wheels), _____

**Check M:** Tell the main ideas at the beginning and at the end of the passage.

**Check SP:** Spell all the words from your notes correctly.

**Check O:** Use your own sentences.

**Check P:** Write more than three paragraphs.

**Check S:** Punctuate sentences correctly.

END OF LESSON 84

Name _____

**A** Complete the outline.

Title: _____

Opinion: _____
_____

Reasons:

1. _____
_____
_____

2. _____
_____
_____

3. _____
_____
_____

(Remind the reader of the opinion.)

These reasons show why _____
_____

# 87

Name _____

## A  Complete the outline.

Title: _____

Opinion: _____
_____

Reasons:

1. _____
_____

2. _____
_____

3. _____
_____

Reminder: What do you want the reader to believe?
_____
_____

## B  Next to each word, write the word that means the opposite.

1. agree _____    3. like _____

2. appear _____   4. honest _____

152   Lesson 87

## C  Write a sentence that tells about the past, the present, and the future.

1. The dogs ran in the yard.

   future  _____

   present _____

2. The bell rings.

   past    _____

   present _____

   future  _____

## D  Put these words in alphabetical order.

1. _____
2. _____
3. _____
4. _____
5. _____
6. _____
7. _____
8. _____
9. _____
10. _____

great
carrot
top
horse
right
visit
elephant
north
jail
millions

**END OF LESSON 87**

# 88 Name _____

**A** Use a prefix to complete each item.

1. arrange   _____   _____
2. join      _____   _____
3. appear    _____   _____
4. charge    _____   _____

**B** Write sentences that tell about the past, the present, and the future.

1. Four children will walk to school.

   past    _____

   present _____

   future  _____

2. The house gets cold.

   past    _____

   present _____

   future  _____

**C** Put these words in alphabetical order.

1. _____
2. _____
3. _____
4. _____
5. _____
6. _____
7. _____
8. _____
9. _____
10. _____

length
bedroom
globe
desk
yellow
raise
should
whole
forest
umbrella

# INDEPENDENT WORK

**D** Label each noun and each adjective.

1. Twelve new books are on that shelf.

2. His brother is running in a race.

3. These hives are full of bees.

4. My favorite dog jumped over the fence.

**END OF LESSON 88**

# 89  Name _____

**A** **Complete the outline.**

Title: _____

Opinion: _____
_____

Reasons:

   1. _____
   _____

   2. _____
   _____

   3. _____
   _____

Reminder: What do you want the reader to believe?
_____

**B. Complete each sentence with an abstract noun.**

1. We are going on vacation next _____.

2. Last night, I had a strange _____.

3. I went to the dentist last _____.

4. Her clever _____ solved the problem.

**C. Use a prefix to complete each item.**

|  | opposite | again |
|---|---|---|
| 1. approve | _____ | _____ |
| 2. arrange | _____ | _____ |
| 3. order | _____ | _____ |
| 4. join | _____ | _____ |
| 5. connect | _____ | _____ |

**D. Write sentences that tell about the past, the present, and the future.**

1. John cleaned the kitchen.

   past _____

   present _____

   future _____

2. Bernie loses his keys.

   past _____

   present _____

   future _____

Lesson 89

### E. Put these words in alphabetical order.

1. _____
2. _____
3. _____
4. _____
5. _____
6. _____

> only
> monkey
> happen
> baby
> answer
> don't

# INDEPENDENT WORK

### F. Complete each sentence with and or but.

1. We were very tired, _____ we had to keep going.

2. The men walked two miles yesterday, _____ they walked two miles today.

3. Roger ate six potatoes, _____ he still wanted more.

4. The car horn sounded, _____ everyone ran away.

**END OF LESSON 89**

**Name** _____

**90**

**A** Complete each sentence with an abstract noun.

1. We didn't laugh at most of her _____ .

2. In the _____ , we'll go swimming.

3. On _____ , we'll have a test.

4. She had enough _____ to lift that box.

**B** In the <u>first</u> blank, write the word that means the <u>opposite</u> of. In the <u>second</u> blank, write the word that means <u>again</u>.

                **opposite**                **again**

1. join _____ _____

2. order _____ _____

3. charge _____ _____

4. connect _____ _____

5. continue _____ _____

Lesson 90

**C** Write sentences that tell about the past, the present, and the future.

1. The cup is on the table.

    past _____

    present _____

    future _____

2. Andy was at home.

    past _____

    present _____

    future _____

# INDEPENDENT WORK

**D** Label each noun and each adjective.

1. These young men are driving home.

2. Five cows were eating in the green field.

3. Roger ate six potatoes.

4. This new car drives easily up the big hill.

Name _____

# 91

## A  Write the word for each description.

1. not clear
   _____

2. not certain
   _____

3. not able
   _____

4. not fair
   _____

## B  Write the word for each description. Use <u>dis</u> or <u>re</u>.

1. opposite of appear
   _____

2. start again
   _____

3. opposite of like
   _____

4. play again
   _____

# INDEPENDENT WORK

## C  Write a sentence that tells about the <u>past</u>, the <u>present</u>, and the <u>future</u>.

- My coat will be warm.

past _____

present _____

future _____

**END OF LESSON 91**

## 92

**A** Put these words in alphabetical order.

1. _____
2. _____
3. _____
4. _____
5. _____
6. _____

- label
- decide
- captain
- enormous
- middle
- forever

**B** Write the correct word for each description.

1. opposite of connect   2. connect again   3. not zipped

_____   _____   _____

4. open again   5. opposite of agree   6. not tied

_____   _____   _____

## INDEPENDENT WORK

**C** Write a sentence that tells about the past, the present, and the future.

- His sister is sad.

past _____

present _____

future _____

**END OF LESSON 92**

# A  Write the word for each description.

1. not healthy

   _____

2. opposite of charge

   _____

3. pay again

   _____

4. not like

   _____

5. open again

   _____

6. opposite of assemble

   _____

# B  Put these words in alphabetical order.

coal
cling
can
curl
cramp

minor
my
mental
moose
made

1. _____
2. _____
3. _____
4. _____
5. _____

**C** Fix up the story using the checks.

|   |   |
|---|---|
|   | Last Saturday morning, Sally was in the |
| WD | kitchen. She washed dishes while her dad was |
|   | shopping for groceries. When Sally heard a |
| Q | knock at the door, she said Who's there?" A |
|   | space creature walked in when the door opened! |
| SP | The space creachure was purple with blue |
|   | hands and great big eyes. Sally had never seen |
|   | anything like it. She said, "You can't come in |
| NP | here." The creature looked sad and said, |
|   | "I need help." |
| N | He told Sally his name was ziggy. He was |
|   | cold, hungry, and felt sick. Sally wrapped a |
| SP | blanket around Ziggy's sholders. Then she made |

164    Lesson 93

**IH** some soup. She took a bowl of soup to Ziggy.

Sally's father couldn't believe his eyes when he got home. He was so shocked that he dropped his bag of groceries. He said, "I don't

**NP** believe this." Sally just smiled and said, "Hi Dad. Meet Ziggy."

**Check WD:** In your first paragraph, tell where the character was and what she was doing.

**Check IH:** In the rest of your paragraphs, tell all the important things that happened—what the characters said and did.

**Check NP:** Start a new paragraph each time a different person talks.

**END OF LESSON 93**

## 94   Name _____

### A  Write the word for each description.

1. without effort  
   _____

2. without a home  
   _____

3. approve again  
   _____

4. opposite of connect  
   _____

5. not zipped  
   _____

6. without a hat  
   _____

### B  Put these words in alphabetical order.

1. _____
2. _____
3. _____
4. _____
5. _____

over

only

often

ocean

ounce

## INDEPENDENT WORK

### C  Write the word for each description.

1. not happy  
   _____

2. make again  
   _____

3. opposite of join  
   _____

4. opposite of qualify  
   _____

5. not ready  
   _____

6. not well  
   _____

**END OF LESSON 94**

**Name** _____

## A  Put these words in alphabetical order.

1. _____
2. _____
3. _____
4. _____
5. _____
6. _____

- squirt
- steep
- scold
- sold
- smiles
- shovel

## B  Write the word for each description.

1. without trees    2. without form    3. tell again
   _____    _____    _____

4. opposite of approve   5. without joints   6. without clouds
   _____    _____    _____

# INDEPENDENT WORK

## C  Write a sentence that tells about the past, the present, and the future.

- We will walk to school.

past _____

present _____

future _____

**END OF LESSON 95**

Lesson 95  167

## A   Put these words in alphabetical order.

1. _____
2. _____
3. _____
4. _____
5. _____
6. _____

bottles
built
blossom
breeze
beetle
billboard

## B   Write the word for each description.

1. full of thought _____
2. opposite of charge _____
3. without roads _____
4. think again _____
5. without care _____
6. full of care _____

# INDEPENDENT WORK

**C** **Complete each sentence with an abstract noun.**

1. In the _____ , I will finish the job.

2. Her great _____ saved three lives.

3. The _____ was the best time ever.

4. I don't have enough _____ to do that.

**D** **Label each underlined noun, pronoun, adjective, and verb. Use N, P, A, and V.**

1. This little girl reads very well.

2. He always gave me an interesting book.

3. Some birds build nests in tall trees.

4. They looked at him with wide eyes.

**END OF LESSON 96**

## 97  Name _____

### A  Put these words in alphabetical order.

1. _____
2. _____
3. _____
4. _____
5. _____
6. _____
7. _____

> change
> cabbage
> dollar
> coast
> decide
> dream
> circus

### B  Write the word for each description.

1. full of harm

   _____

2. opposite of pleased

   _____

3. without a voice

   _____

4. light again

   _____

5. without joy

   _____

6. full of joy

   _____

# INDEPENDENT WORK

**C** Put these words in alphabetical order.

1. _____
2. _____
3. _____
4. _____
5. _____
6. _____
7. _____
8. _____

> eraser
> enormous
> edge
> easy
> evening
> escape
> eggs
> eyes

**END OF LESSON 97**

## 98 Name _____

**A** Put these words in alphabetical order.

1. _____
2. _____
3. _____
4. _____
5. _____
6. _____
7. _____

thought
ruler
tenth
rich
taste
rough
return

# INDEPENDENT WORK

**B** Write the word for each description.

1. full of hurt _____

2. do again _____

3. not happy _____

4. without a home _____

5. without sense _____

6. full of grace _____

7. read again _____

8. without cheer _____

**C** Write a sentence that tells about the past, the present, and the future.

- Henry will see the mailman arrive.

past _____

present _____

future _____

**END OF LESSON 98**

## 99    Name _____

**A** Put these words in alphabetical order.

1. _____
2. _____
3. _____
4. _____
5. _____
6. _____
7. _____

- middle
- island
- machine
- insist
- mummy
- money
- idea

# INDEPENDENT WORK

**B** Write the word for each description.

1. write again  _____
2. full of fear  _____
3. without fear  _____
4. opposite of agree  _____
5. not willing  _____
6. full of help  _____
7. start again  _____
8. without end  _____

**END OF LESSON 99**

# Name

## A  Put these words in alphabetical order.

1. _____
2. _____
3. _____
4. _____
5. _____
6. _____

> flower
> juggle
> football
> fence
> fifty
> join

# INDEPENDENT WORK

## B  Write the word for each description.

1. full of truth
   _____

2. without trees
   _____

3. not certain
   _____

4. light again
   _____

5. without care
   _____

6. not stable
   _____

7. play again
   _____

8. opposite of qualify
   _____

Lesson 100   175

**C** Complete each sentence with an abstract noun.

1. He learns quickly because he has a good _____ .

2. We will be done with the project next _____ .

3. I have plenty of _____ to do that job.

4. Roger told a funny _____ .

**D** Label each underlined noun, pronoun, adjective, and verb. Use P, N, A, and V.

1. My big brother came home after he fixed his bike.

2. They sometimes go for a short walk before dinner.

3. Work quickly so we can get the job finished.

4. Val gave him a funny book about animals.

**END OF LESSON 100**

Name _____

## A   Put these words in alphabetical order.

1. _____
2. _____
3. _____
4. _____
5. _____
6. _____
7. _____

- thirsty
- notice
- twice
- terrible
- neither
- traffic
- toast

## B   Label each adverb.

- Some sentences end with an **adverb**.
- Adverbs tell **how,** or **when,** or **where.**

Sample sentence 1:   The workers moved dirt.

Sample sentence 2:   The workers moved quickly.

1. The dogs barked yesterday.
2. The girls walked away.
3. The scientists watched animals.
4. The little boy yelled loudly.
5. My mother bought milk.
6. The hunters watched birds.
7. Her eyes looked up.
8. Tracy travelled alone.

**C** Write the word for each description.

1. being hard _____

2. being tender _____

3. opposite of belief _____

4. full of thought _____

5. without thought _____

6. being bright _____

7. not happy _____

8. without a point _____

# INDEPENDENT WORK

**D** Label each noun and each adjective.

1. Our favorite animal is a horse.

2. Six new books are on the top shelf.

3. These boys are planting two trees.

4. One day I hope to be a great teacher.

**END OF LESSON 101**

**Name** _____

## A  Put these words in alphabetical order.

1. _____
2. _____
3. _____
4. _____
5. _____
6. _____
7. _____
8. _____
9. _____
10. _____

> ruler
> airplane
> done
> knives
> thumb
> dinner
> ceiling
> report
> honest
> weather

## B  Write the word for each description.

1. write again
   _____

2. being fair
   _____

3. opposite of agree
   _____

4. not finished
   _____

5. without hope
   _____

6. being fresh
   _____

7. being close
   _____

8. without a coat
   _____

Lesson 102  179

**C** Label each adverb.

1. The girls had adventures.
2. The boys will play tomorrow.
3. The ducks splashed water.
4. The children sang songs.
5. The children sang loudly.
6. The dessert came later.
7. Healthy babies grow quickly.
8. My uncle loves watermelon.

**END OF LESSON 102**

Name _____

**A  Put these words in alphabetical order.**

1. _____
2. _____
3. _____
4. _____
5. _____
6. _____
7. _____
8. _____
9. _____
10. _____

> banana
> electric
> special
> amaze
> decide
> plastic
> people
> early
> hundred
> purple

**B  Label each adverb.**

1. That man talks fast.

2. Her brother ate dessert.

3. She will meet with us tomorrow.

4. She washed the dog slowly.

5. His dog chewed on a bone.

6. Greg uses a shovel well.

7. Sally did her homework.

Lesson 103   181

## C  Write the word for each description.

1. one who rides

2. being sad

3. full of thought

4. opposite of approve

5. one who runs

6. without joy

7. being dull

8. not done

9. without sleeves

10. build again

## D  Write each sentence so it begins with the part that can be moved.

1. We will be very happy if we win the game.

2. She will win the race unless she falls down.

3. The field was dry although it rained all night.

**END OF LESSON 103**

**Name** _____

**104**

### A  Put these words in alphabetical order.

1. _____    8. _____
2. _____    9. _____
3. _____    10. _____
4. _____
5. _____
6. _____
7. _____

shadow
lemon
giant
visit
destroy
great
younger
bread
space
globe

### B  Label the adverb in each sentence. Then circle how, when, or where.

1. They walked far.                          how    when    where

2. They walked together.                     how    when    where

3. They walked daily.                        how    when    where

4. They looked everywhere.                   how    when    where

5. The girls sat quietly.                    how    when    where

6. Al and his brother worked yesterday.      how    when    where

Lesson 104    183

**C** Write the word for each description.

1. type again

2. being mean

3. wash again

4. one who washes

5. one who bakes

6. without taste

7. full of skill

8. being round

9. without care

10. one who tastes

**END OF LESSON 104**

**Name** _____ 105

**A** | **If an item is a sentence, circle the subject and underline the predicate.**

1. Before the rain stopped.

2. Stood on top of the table.

3. She caught a bug.

4. Mary sat down.

5. Mary, Tom, and their dog.

6. After the show.

Lesson 105 **185**

**B** Put these words in alphabetical order.

1. _____
2. _____
3. _____
4. _____
5. _____
6. _____
7. _____
8. _____

count
collar
complete
cob
cod
coat
cone
cook

**C** Write the word for each description.

1. being hard
2. one who thinks
3. being cold
4. one who works
5. opposite of colored

6. color again
7. full of tears
8. without tears
9. being bright
10. not healthy

186    Lesson 105

**D** Label the adverb in each sentence. Then circle how, when, or where.

1. His brother didn't walk **well**.      how    when    where

2. The men in suits talked **loudly**.     how    when    where

3. The door opened very **slowly**.     how    when    where

4. Three girls arrived **late**.     how    when    where

5. Those packages will be delivered **soon**.     how    when    where

6. Five horses ran **everywhere**.     how    when    where

**END OF LESSON 105**

**106** Name _____

**A** Put these words in alphabetical order.

1. _____
2. _____
3. _____
4. _____
5. _____
6. _____

- dry
- driver
- draft
- dream
- drop
- drum

**B** If an item is a sentence, circle the subject and underline the predicate.

1. After we finished eating.   _____

2. He opened it.   _____

3. A shirt, blue jeans, and shoes.   _____

4. Before the snow stopped.   _____

5. She jumped up.   _____

### C  Write the word for each description.

1. one who sits  
   _____

2. being narrow  
   _____

3. without pain  
   _____

4. being firm  
   _____

5. think again  
   _____

6. not firm  
   _____

7. one who gives  
   _____

8. give again  
   _____

9. without water  
   _____

10. one who speaks  
    _____

# INDEPENDENT WORK

### D  Underline the adverb in each sentence. Then circle how, when, or where.

1. Robert walked upstairs.      how    when    where
2. My uncle sings loudly.      how    when    where
3. I ran my best race yesterday.      how    when    where
4. He said, "It won't last forever."      how    when    where
5. Amy cried softly.      how    when    where

**END OF LESSON 106**

# 107   Name _____

**A** Cross out the words that don't come between <u>cents</u> and <u>cops</u>. Write the other words in alphabetical order.

1. _____
2. _____
3. _____
4. _____
5. _____

> cents        cops
> can
> cup
> certain
> chip
> circus
> clipper
> call
> city

**B** If an item is a sentence, circle the subject and underline the predicate.

1. Before we went to sleep.   _____

2. She helped him.   _____

3. When they got home.   _____

4. A truck, a car, and a motorcycle.   _____

5. He stopped talking.   _____

# INDEPENDENT WORK

**C** Rewrite each sentence so it begins with the part that can be moved. Remember the comma.

1. They will have fun if they work together.

   _____
   _____

2. I can't go to the movies unless I finish my chores.

   _____
   _____

3. He brought a cake although he almost dropped the plate.

   _____
   _____

**D** Write the word for each description.

1. one who plays          _____
2. one who washes         _____
3. not washed             _____
4. being light            _____
5. opposite of agree      _____
6. without a clue         _____
7. one who speaks         _____

**END OF LESSON 107**

# 108  Name _____

## A  Cross out the words that don't come between <u>chief</u> and <u>clean</u>. Write the other words in alphabetical order.

**chief     clean**

~~circle~~ circle
~~chill~~ chill
~~chew~~
~~chirp~~ chirp
~~copy~~
~~chin~~ chin
~~chunk~~ chunk
~~class~~ class
~~claw~~ claw

1. chill
2. chin
3. chirp
4. chunk
5. circle
6. class
7. claw

## B  Complete each item using one of the words in the list.

**create     creation     creator     creature**

1. Her last _____ was a washing machine with three tubs.

2. He was a talented artist. He could _____ very good pictures.

3. Next to the horse was a strange looking _____ with a long tail.

4. She was the _____ of Wonder World Park.

**C** Write words to complete each sentence. Make an arrowhead to show where the words go in each sentence.

|  |  |
|---|---|
|  | Clem didn't talk much so his teammates |
| **CS** | thought that he wasn't very smart. One day, |
|  | surprised them by making up a new way to |
|  | score. His teammates tried out Clem's plan and |
| **CS** | they beat a very good team. They that Clem |
|  | was the smartest player on the team. |

**Check CS:** Write complete sentences.

# INDEPENDENT WORK

**D** Underline the adverb in each sentence. Then circle <u>how</u>, <u>when</u>, or <u>where</u>.

1. I hope I will finish the job tomorrow.     how    when    where

2. He always works quickly.    how    when    where

3. My mom taught me to write neatly.    how    when    where

4. When we saw the snow, we ran outside.    how    when    where

**END OF LESSON 108**

## 109

**A** Complete each item using one of the words in the box.

> vision    visible    invisible    visibility

1. The _____ was better on Tuesday than it was on Monday.

2. Only some of the people were _____ in the distance.

3. Martha wore glasses, but Joanne had perfect _____ .

4. He was so embarrassed he wished he was _____ .

**B** For items 3 and 4, write all the letters that words on the page could begin with.

1. caretaker        gardener

2. friends          holiday

3. buns             fix          _____

4. telephone        word         _____

# INDEPENDENT WORK

**C** If an item is a sentence, circle the subject and underline the predicate. If an item is not a sentence, write a sentence that uses the words in the item.

1. His uncle and two cousins. _____

2. Before the storm was over. _____

3. His mother agreed. _____

4. Bought the complete set of books. _____

5. Before the sun set, they finished eating. _____

**END OF LESSON 109**

**110**   Name _____

### A  Use your glossary to answer each question.

1. What are the guide words for the word **insist**?

   _____

2. What are the guide words for the word **reef**?

   _____

# INDEPENDENT WORK

### B  Underline the adverb in each sentence. Then circle how, when, or where.

1. I learned that moles live underground.     how   when   where

2. Mary will eat later.     how   when   where

3. My mom called for Billy to come inside.     how   when   where

4. Julio stepped on the ice carefully.     how   when   where

5. Sally said she didn't feel well.     how   when   where

196   Lesson 110

## C. Write the word for each description.

1. without stars  _____
2. not seen  _____
3. one who reads  _____
4. being tough  _____

## D. If an item is a sentence, circle the subject and underline the predicate. If the item is not a sentence, write a sentence that uses the words in the item.

1. We didn't agree.  _____
   _____

2. He would always put his fork.  _____
   _____

3. Looked for three hours before going home.  _____
   _____

4. He is one smart boy.  _____
   _____

5. Her room and the stairs next to it.  _____
   _____

6. They drove yesterday.  _____
   _____

**END OF LESSON 110**

**111** Name _____

**A** For each item, write the guide words for the page in your glossary where you would find the word.

**Guide Words**

1. familiar    _____    _____

2. comment    _____    _____

3. peer    _____    _____

# INDEPENDENT WORK

**B** Write a good sentence that uses the part that is shown.

1. unless we get up before seven

   _____
   _____

2. although he doesn't smile much

   _____
   _____

3. if the wind stops blowing

   _____
   _____

**END OF LESSON 111**

Name _____

## A  Write the best word to complete each sentence.

> additional    add    addition

1. We need to _____ salt to the stew.

2. The curtains are a good _____ to the living room.

3. We invited five _____ people to the party.

## B  Complete each sentence.

1. Her mother was happy before _____

2. Ann was happy because _____

3. Rosa was happy while _____

## C  For each item, write the guide words for the page in your glossary where you would find the word.

**Guide Words**

1. success     _____     _____

2. musher      _____     _____

3. beware      _____     _____

**END OF LESSON 112**

Lesson 112   199

## A  Write the best word to complete each sentence.

> reflect     reflector     reflection

1. The bird looked at its _____ in the puddle.

2. Todd had five _____ on his bike.

3. His old shoes were dull, and didn't _____ light.

## B  Complete each sentence using a word from the list.

> because     after     when

1. Bill went to the doctor _____
   _____

> before     after     while

2. Their car broke down _____
   _____

**C** For each item, write the guide words for the page in your glossary where you would find the word.

**Guide Words**

1. dedicated  _____    _____
2. weary      _____    _____
3. thorough   _____    _____

**D** Find the meaning of the red words in an online dictionary.

1. The **laboratory** had many test tubes and flasks.

2. A **blimp** has an oval shape.

# INDEPENDENT WORK

**E** Write the words that come between <u>handy</u> and <u>hurt</u> in alphabetical order.

1. _____
2. _____
3. _____
4. _____
5. _____
6. _____

**handy     hurt**
   hidden
   hair
   hoard
   hummed
   hear
   heater
   hush
   home

**END OF LESSON 113**

Lesson 113   201

**A** Draw a line from each part of speech to the correct definition.

1. pronoun • • tells how, when, or where

2. adverb • • replaces a noun

3. verb • • names a person, place, or thing

4. adjective • • tells what kind or how many

5. noun • • tells what somebody or something does

# INDEPENDENT WORK

**B** Label each underlined noun, pronoun, and verb. Use N, P, and V.

1. Her face turned red when she took a bow.

2. They always eat apples after lunch.

3. Walk quickly and arrive at school early.

4. Mary showed me a large picture of her.

END OF LESSON 116

Name _____

**A** Draw a line from each part of speech to the correct definition.

1. verb • • replaces a noun

2. noun • • tells how, when, or where

3. pronoun • • tells what kind or how many

4. adverb • • tells what somebody or something does

5. adjective • • names a person, place, or thing

**B** Find the meaning of the underlined words in your glossary.

1. The old window was no longer <u>transparent</u>.

2. She was smart and had a lot of <u>confidence</u>.

3. Climbing that hill is a <u>piece of cake</u> for me.

4. She is a <u>top-notch</u> car mechanic.

END OF LESSON 117

# 118

**A** Complete each sentence with a word that makes sense.

> A. busy   sleepy   old   handsome   ugly   young
>    little   big   happy   sad   brown   lonely

> B. now   later   slowly   quickly   always   sometimes
>    loudly   quietly   often   never   sadly   gladly

1. He moved _____ .

2. Their doghouse was _____ .

3. My mother was walking _____ .

4. Everybody got up _____ .

5. Their farm was _____ .

6. Her brother is _____ .

**B** Label the black words.

> **N** for nouns  **A** for adjectives
> **P** for pronouns  **AV** for adverbs
> **V** for verbs

1. Robert ran quickly to the long table.

2. A fat cat smiled at the butterfly.

3. Those children sang after they ate lunch.

**C** Find the meaning of the underlined words in your glossary.

1. If you insist on leaving early, I'll go with you.

2. The horizon was bright pink.

3. It takes a long time to become a veterinarian.

4. His car was on its last legs.

**END OF LESSON 118**

## 119  Name _____

**A**  Complete each sentence with a word that makes sense.

> A. busy    sleepy    old    handsome    ugly    young
> little    big    happy    sad    lonely    soft
> comfortable    unusual    hot    cold

> B. now    later    slowly    quickly    always    sometimes
> loudly    quietly    often    never    sadly    gladly    gently

1. The tallest building looks _____.

2. Her bicycle could go _____.

3. My dad works _____.

4. The pillow feels _____.

5. Donna is very _____.

**B**  Find the meaning of the underlined words in your glossary.

1. She will <u>plunge</u> into the pool.

2. The coach <u>congratulated</u> the winning team.

3. They walked <u>briskly</u> up the hill.

4. After that hike, I have to <u>hit the sack</u>.

**C** Label the black words.

> **N** for nouns  **A** for adjectives
> **P** for pronouns  **AV** for adverbs
> **V** for verbs

1. He followed them to the park.

2. Fran sat quietly under the old tree.

3. Mom gave her two hugs yesterday.

**D** Find the meaning of the red words in an online dictionary.

1. I'll be there, rain or shine.

2. The drug has no side effects.

END OF LESSON 119

### 120 Name _____

**A** Label the black words.

> N for nouns  A for adjectives
> P for pronouns  AV for adverbs
> V for verbs

1. The red car started quickly on a cold day.

2. The tallest girl was the leader today.

**B** Find the meaning of the underlined words in your glossary.

1. After Robert was rude, Alice gave him the cold shoulder.

2. Be careful what you say or you'll spill the beans.

3. A lot of bikers get cold feet before going down that hill.

208  Lesson 120

**C** **Complete each sentence with a word that makes sense.**

A. busy   sleepy   old   handsome   ugly   young
little   big   happy   sad   lonely   soft
hard   comfortable   unusual   hot   cold

B. now   later   slowly   quickly   always   sadly
sometimes   loudly   quietly   often   never

1. His brother talked _____ .

2. Their couch is _____ .

3. Tom will read _____ .

4. Her shoes looked _____ .

5. The weather is going to be _____ .

**END OF LESSON 120**

**A** **Complete each sentence.**

1. Rosa is shorter than _____ .

2. The shortest child is _____ .

3. Hans is shorter than _____ and _____ .

Name _____

**A** Use a dictionary to find the correct meaning of each word that is unfamiliar. Circle the correct meaning.

1. Her answer was concise.
   - short    • silly    • interesting

2. Hoping to find my ring, I checked every particle of sand.
   - bag    • pile    • speck

3. Don't be mulish.
   - slow    • stubborn    • late

4. Waiting for the letter to arrive was agony.
   - torture    • fun    • exciting

5. The writer of this book is anonymous.
   - famous    • rich    • unknown

**B** Complete the research on your group's planet today.

Mercury    Venus    Earth    Mars

END OF LESSON 123

## 128

**A** Write the best word to complete each simile.

1. He moved very slowly.

   He moved like a _____

   - hawk    • tree    • turtle

2. His arms were very skinny.

   His arms were like _____

   - tree trunks    • sticks    • posts

3. His mother is very old.

   She looks like a _____

   - prune    • peacock    • pansy

4. The valley was very hot.

   The valley was as hot as _____

   - a furnace    • a lake    • an icicle

**END OF LESSON 128**

Name _____  **129**

### A  Write the best word to complete each simile.

1. His hands were very rough.

   His hands were like _____

   - paper towels  • ice  • sandpaper

2. Mary's teeth are very white.

   Her teeth are as white as _____

   - stones  • pearls  • pears

3. His muscles were very hard.

   His muscles were as hard as _____

   - roots  • mountains  • rocks

4. They ran very fast.

   They ran like _____

   - the weather  • the wind  • the winters

### B  Use a dictionary. Find the correct spelling. Then circle it.

1. another  
   unother

2. wimen  
   women

Lesson 129    213

## C  Write the letter of the correct list in each box. Then complete each item.

**A:** more slowly  more sadly  more wildly  more beautifully  more quietly

**B:** most gently  most quietly  most sadly  most wildly  most quickly

**C:** happier  funnier  bigger  older  taller  louder  cleaner

**D:** sweetest  hungriest  loudest  shortest  oldest  poorest  happiest  smallest  tallest

1. The elm tree was the _____ on the block.

2. The gray horse runs _____ than the white horse.

3. Jan has always been _____ than her brother.

4. The black dog runs the _____ .

5. Robert sings _____ than anybody else.

6. Fran is the _____ girl in the class.

**END OF LESSON 129**

**Name** _____  130

**A** For each sentence, write the letter of the picture that shows the right meaning.

1. She swept the front <u>stoop</u>. ___

2. Don't <u>stoop</u> so much when you walk. ___

3. Somebody should <u>crop</u> the bushes next to the driveway. ___

4. In August, we harvest the corn <u>crop</u>. ___

A

B

C

D

**B** Write the best word to complete each simile.

1. She was as tall as _____
   - a sidewalk
   - a pole
   - a child

2. Her fingernails were like _____
   - claws
   - bunnies
   - carrots

3. He was as strong as _____
   - sand
   - a bull
   - a mouse

4. The package was as light as _____
   - a cat
   - boots
   - a feather

**END OF LESSON 130**

**A** **Work each item.**

1. Write the date for the fifth day of August in the year 1968.

   _____

2. Write the date for the third day of June in the year 2001.

   _____

3. Write the date for the eleventh day of March in the year 1792.

   _____

4. Write the date for the eighth day of July in the year 1812.

   _____

5. Write the date for the nineteenth day of November in the year 2011.

   _____

**B** **Put the words in order from the strongest belief to the weakest belief.**

think    wonder    suspect    know

1. _____

2. _____

3. _____

4. _____

**C** Write the best word to complete each simile.

1. The lake was as smooth as _____.
   - glass   • water   • sunshine

2. He had a mind like _____.
   - a foot   • a head   • a computer

3. Her eyes got as round as _____.
   - ears   • saucers   • buckets

4. She was as pretty as _____.
   - a pin   • a picture   • a pine

# INDEPENDENT WORK

**D** Write the word for each description.

1. being gentle _____

2. full of joy _____

3. without fear _____

4. one who paints _____

5. not cooked _____

6. do again _____

**END OF LESSON 131**

## A  Work each item.

1. Write the date for the 21st day of May in the year 1886.

   _____

2. Write the date for the seventeenth day of September in the year 2010.

   _____

3. Write the date for the tenth day of January in the year 1935.

   _____

4. Write the date for the 23rd day of March in the year 1722.

   _____

## B  Write the correct word for each sentence.

> wondered    knew    suspected    thought

1. The lawnmower was not in the garage, and John didn't know where it was. He _____ what had happened to it.

2. John knew that he took off his coat and put it some place. He knew he didn't put his coat in the kitchen or his room. He _____ it could be in the living room.

3. The policeman asked John what his name was and other things he _____ .

4. John worked for nearly an hour on the math problem, but he _____ that his answer might be wrong.

**C** **Replace the underlined parts with similes.**

Once upon a time, there was a beautiful princess named Sarah. Her hair was very black. Her eyes were very blue. Princess Sarah lived in a castle on top of a mountain. But Sarah didn't want to stay in the castle. So she escaped. She had to be very quiet, and she had to be very brave. She crept out of the castle and jumped on her horse, Radar. Radar ran very fast. Sarah rode to the nearest village where she found her Uncle John.

When he heard Sarah's secret, his eyes became big and round. He could hardly believe her story. But he knew she was telling the truth. He was very strong, so he was able to help her go back to the castle and catch the bat that sat under her hat!

| wind | mouse | saucer | sky | coal | ocean |
| lion | moon | ox | dragon | night | spider |

**END OF LESSON 132**

Name _____

**133**

### A  For each sentence, write the letter of the picture that shows the right meaning.

1. He had a stack of <u>bills</u> in his wallet. ___

2. The bird used its <u>bill</u> to weave a nest. ___

3. The <u>light</u> was so poor that we could hardly see things. ___

4. The bubbles were so <u>light</u> that they floated with the wind. ___

A.                 B.                 C.                 D.

### B  Write the correct word for each sentence.

| knew | thought | suspected | wondered |

1. I _____ I had painted the wall the right color, but the next day, the wall looked too dark.

2. The others weren't sure where Hanner Park was, but I had gone there many times and _____ how to get there.

3. I found a candy bar wrapper all torn up in the bedroom. Our dog was sleeping on the bed. So I _____ that she had eaten the candy bar.

4. They just told us that we would have a new teacher next week. I _____ who it would be.

**END OF LESSON 133**

## 134

**A** Complete each sentence.

• He got out of bed and went downstairs.

1. He _____ out of bed and _____ downstairs.

2. He _____ out of bed and _____ downstairs.

3. He _____ out of bed and _____ downstairs.

• snuck / crept      • jumped / ran      • crawled / limped

**B** Replace each contraction with a word pair.

The students weren't ready for the quiz. The teacher hadn't told the class that they'd have to write about foods they don't like to eat. There wasn't anything that Charley didn't like to eat. So he couldn't write anything.

**END OF LESSON 134**

Name _____

## A  Complete each sentence.

> - He turned around and spoke to her.
> - He looked over and talked to her.

1. He _____ and _____ her.

2. He _____ and _____ her.

3. He _____ and _____ her.

- shivered / begged
- smiled / whispered to
- frowned / yelled at

## B  Make a line from the description to the correct word.

1. You're pretty sure you'll do well.          •     •  anxious

2. You are nervous and worried.               •     •  curious

3. You are really happy about something.      •     •  confident

4. You want to know more.                     •     •  excited

Lesson 135

**C** **Replace each contraction with a word pair.**

Our windows weren't clean, so my dad told my brother and me that we'd have to clean them. We couldn't reach the top of the windows, so we didn't clean those parts.

Dad asked, "Where's the step ladder?"

I said, "We don't know."

Then Dad said, "Who's going to look for it?"

I said, "I'll do that."

Dad said, "Then he's the one who's going to finish the windows." So I found the ladder, and my brother finished the job.

### D  Write the address with commas.

1. Greenville Iowa

   _____

2. Street number: 45
   Street name: Vine Street
   City name: Greenville
   State name: Iowa

   _____

3. Street number: 7
   Street name: Old Goat Road
   City name: Chico
   State name: California

   _____

### E  Draw a line from each expression to what it means.

1. She slept like a log last night.  •          •  She was tough.

2. She was really hard-nosed.  •          •  She talked a lot.

3. Well, I'll be a monkey's uncle.  •          •  She slept very soundly.

4. She talked until she was blue in the face.  •          •  The person was really surprised.

**END OF LESSON 135**

# 136

**A** Complete each sentence.

> angrily    excitedly    usually    wearily

1. "I can't wait to see the mountains!" he said _____.

2. "I'm so tired I can hardly move," he said _____.

3. "Get out of here right now!" he said _____.

**B** Draw a line from each expression to what it means.

1. He was always walking on thin ice.
2. It was raining cats and dogs.
3. He was really hard-nosed.
4. He could have been knocked over by a feather.
5. He slept like a log.
6. He always does best when his back is against the wall.

- He slept very soundly.
- He was really surprised.
- He was tough.
- He does best when he faces serious problems.
- It was raining very hard.
- He was always doing dangerous things.

**C** **Replace each contraction with word pairs.**

I'm writing this email to complain about the dishwasher you sold me. It doesn't work. Here's what happened. At first, I couldn't turn it on. The on button wouldn't work. It's on now, but it's not working right. It doesn't clean the dishes well. That's why I'm asking for my money back.

**END OF LESSON 136**

## 137  Name _____

**A** Complete each sentence.

> happily    sadly    wearily    angrily    awkwardly

1. "I'm so sorry for breaking your glasses," he said _____.

2. "Wow, this is a great surprise!" she said _____.

3. "I can't . . . I can't find the right words," she said _____.

4. "I can't stand this place," he said _____.

**B** Cross out the improper words. Then write the correct words above.

> give me    police officer    children    surprised    people    dollars

1. Those little kids love to play with me.

2. Six guys helped me clean up the beach.

3. I was blown away when they said I had won.

4. Maria needed five more bucks for the game.

5. A cop stopped our car.

6. Who will gimme some extra pizza?

**C** **Draw a line from each expression to what it means.**

1. She got cold feet before she went on stage. • • She tried to do things she couldn't do.

2. Her homework was a piece of cake. • • There was no doubt that we would win.

3. The victory was in the bag. • • She was nervous before she performed.

4. She bit off more than she could chew. • • It was very easy work.

# INDEPENDENT WORK

**D** **Draw a line from each description to the correct word.**

1. Being really happy about something. • • confident

2. Being nervous or worried. • • curious

3. Wanting to know more. • • excited

4. Being pretty sure you'll do well. • • anxious

**END OF LESSON 137**

## 138  Name _____

### A  Cross out the improper words. Then write the correct words above.

> bad experience   food   leave   dollars   movie

1. My mom always fixes great grub.

2. How many bucks do you have with you?

3. We loved that flick!

4. Going to the hospital every month is a bummer.

5. We need to split from the game early.

### B  Underline each sentence that means exactly what it says.

1. Her homework was a piece of cake.

   Her dessert was a piece of cake.

2. After going ice skating, he had cold feet.

   Before going on stage, he had cold feet.

3. Four apples are in the bag.

   Winning our next game is in the bag.

4. At work, he bit off more than he could chew.

   At lunchtime, he bit off more than he could chew.

**END OF LESSON 138**

Name _____

# 139

## A   Cross out the improper words. Then write the proper words above.

> disgusting    relax    noise    leave    potatoes

1. I wish they'd stop making that racket.

2. What's the best way to cook these taters?

3. The yard looked gross with garbage everywhere.

4. My little brother needs to chill.

5. Todd told us it was time to split.

## B   Underline each sentence that means exactly what it says.

1. She thought that her new job would be a piece of cake.
   She thought that the piece of cake was too big for her to eat.

2. Billy wore his summer shoes and got cold feet.
   Jan told us she would lead the singing but she got cold feet.

3. I didn't think we could do it, but my brother said it was in the bag.
   There wasn't room for all the items to fit in the bag.

4. I always make sure I don't bite off more than I can chew.
   Everything looked so tasty that I bit off more than I could chew.

**END OF LESSON 139**

## 140

**A** Cross out the improper words. Then write the proper words above.

We weren't sure what we'd do after lunch, but we knew we had to get away from the racket. Two guys were fixing a problem on the roof. Water had made gross damp marks in the ceiling. We needed to split. Anna wanted to go get some grub. I wanted to see a flick, but Ryan just wanted to chill and talk. We only had 12 bucks, so there wasn't enough for the flicks. We bought some grub at the cheapest place in town and walked to the mall.

**B** Underline each sentence that means exactly what it says.

1. She tore her sleeve during the game and had a very cold shoulder.

   For more than a week, I was mad at Harry and gave him the cold shoulder.

2. The shower didn't work well, and he couldn't get much hot water.

   He borrowed his brother's sweater and really got in hot water for doing it.

3. We discussed the problem for more than ten minutes, but we're still not on the same page.

   I was reading the part that was on page 88, but our teacher was not on the same page.

**END OF LESSON 140**

Name _____

**TEST 1**

**1** **Put in the missing capitals and periods.**

My older sister took her dog to the park her dog chased a skunk the skunk got mad it made a terrible stink my sister had to wash her dog for hours to get rid of the smell

**2** **Edit the passage so no sentences begin with And or And Then.**

Linda and Milly wanted to row Linda's boat around the lake. And they tried to pull the boat down the hill, but the boat didn't move. And then the girls tried to push the boat down the hill, but it still didn't move. So Linda went to a house near the lake to ask for help.

The woman at the house said the girls could use her horse to pull the boat to the lake. And then the girls led the horse to the boat and tied the boat to the horse. And the horse pulled the boat to the lake.

**3** **Edit the sentences so they tell what happened.**

| had | picked | ate | gave | filled | spelled |

1. He was giving me a pen.

2. He was eating a banana.

3. They were picking flowers.

4. He is filling the glass.

5. My friend is having a party.

6. A boy was spelling words.

**END OF TEST 1**

# Name _____

**TEST 2**

**1** Write complete sentences that tell what the people said.

1. Edgar said, _____

_____

2. _____

_____

3. _____

_____

TEST 2

**2** Write a paragraph about the pictures. Write at least one sentence for each number.

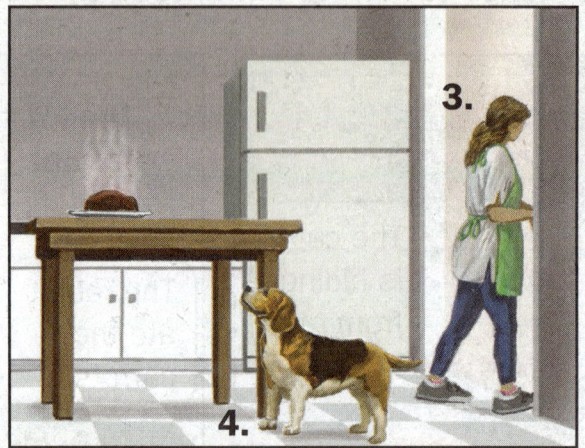
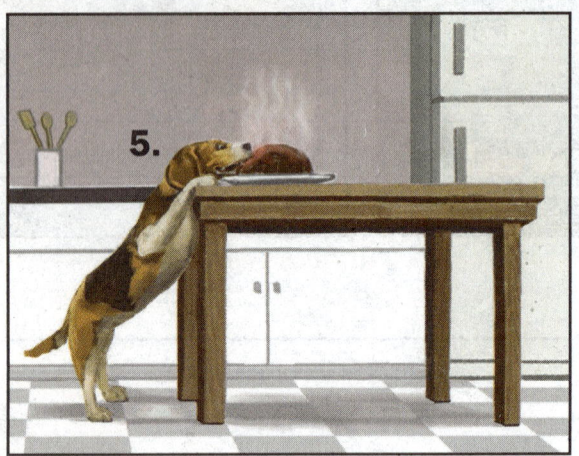

| kitchen | roast | oven | howl | table |

**Check IH:** Did you tell all the important things that happened?

**Check CP:** Does each sentence begin with a capital letter and end with a period?

**Check DID:** Does each sentence tell what somebody or something **did**?

Mastery Test 2

**END OF TEST 2**

**TEST 3**

Name _____

**1** The number after each item tells how many mistakes are in the item. Fix up the mistakes.

1. Marias dog chased two cats up a tree (2)

2. The babies fell asleep on anns bed. (2)

3. Mr. adams said "I liked that book. (3)

4. Grace met Lindas brother he was very tall. (3)

5. He said my team won the game. (4)

**2** Write a sentence for each item. Tell what Hiro said and what Heather said.

1. _____

2. _____

**END OF TEST 3**

Mastery Test 3    T-7

Name _____

# TEST 4

**1** Write a paragraph that tells about the first picture and the missing picture in the display.

> clothesline     dried     clothes     climb
> water     campsite     blanket

Tom went camping next to a cold mountain stream.

**Check IH:** Tell the important things that happened in the first picture and the middle picture.

**Check Q:** Correctly punctuate the sentence that tells what Tom said.

**Check S:** Write all your sentences correctly (CP, SP, DID).

Mastery Test 4

END OF TEST 4